To Collen

I Am Not My

Reversing the Irreversible

Thank you for reading & your continued support xx

04.12.21

I Am Not My Diagnosis:

Reversing the Irreversible

Carley Mellors-Blair

BSc (hons) MRSM MFHT

Edited by

Christine Latimer

I Am Not My Diagnosis: Reversing the Irreversible

First published in Great Britain by Altered Health Solutions Ltd 2021

Altered Health Solutions Ltd
6-8 The Market Place
Nottingham
NG5 6ND

www.alteredhealth.co.uk

ISBN 978-1-7398874-3-8

Dedication

I dedicate this book to everyone who has shaped my journey so far; those who put blocks in my path and those who propelled me forward, to the energy draining people and those who were energy fountains. Without all of you I wouldn't be the woman I am growing into today.

And to all those people I am yet to touch in some way, welcome. I dedicate these words to your power, your strength, and your readiness to take full responsibility for your health and wellbeing. I pray that my energy through this book ignites you to own your brilliance and your magic, and to begin living the life that you were actually born to live.

#borntoheal

Your partner in health

Carley

To my sons Mallique and Matthaus thank you for choosing me.
I love you xx

Table of Contents

Foreword

I once had a conversation with an oncology consultant after he attended a lecture I'd given on the mind-body connection. In his experience, he explained, one of the most important factors in recovery from not only cancer (which is his own field) but from a large number of other medical conditions, is will power, a total determination to find a way to get better.

Of course, this doesn't mean that if a person doesn't recover quickly from something that they weren't determined. There can be a large number of factors that feed into any person's experience. But on the whole, he explained, determination often finds a way even when there doesn't seem to be a way. Determination knocks down the door when it seems locked, or it finds a back door. Determination finds solutions that don't seem to exist at face value. Determination searches the spaces that others walk past, it sees the pattern in chaos, it finds the light amid the shadow.

Carley Mellors-Blair has determination in abundance. Despite the numerous challenges and setbacks she's known, her determination to find a way through is what got her to the place she's in today – healthy, vibrant, successful, and a shining light to many who call upon her for guidance.

Carley changed her prognosis by changing herself. She changed her mindset, her lifestyle, and especially her nutritional intake. Even in the face of some resistance from family and friends, she cut out all foods that were detrimental to her health and began to consume only those that would benefit her. The results were transformational.

I've known transformation when I radically changed my diet too, so I find these changes that Carley made particularly interesting. For most of my life, I only saw food as fuel. Neither my parents nor their parents had ever been taught anything else.

But almost 20 years ago, after attending a lecture on nutrition, I made some significant changes in my life. I cut out diary, increased fruits, vegetables and salads, and dramatically reduced my sugar intake. Dairy was actually the most difficult for me. My partner had often joked that I drank 'baby tea', that is, tea with a massive amount of milk such that it barely had the colour tea at all. I also drank a mug of latte every day as I tend to do much of my writing work in coffee shops.

But I persevered with tea and coffee without milk, armed with the knowledge that taste buds renew in around 2-3 weeks. Low and behold, three weeks into things and I was actually loving the taste of tea and coffee without milk. I've never looked back.

Over the course of 8 weeks of my new lifestyle, I also lost around 20 pounds in weight. I wasn't trying to lose weight, nor did I think I needed to. It was merely the side effect of eating more healthily. Friends noted the difference in my skin tone too.

I've maintained a healthy diet ever since – more or less. I try my best, but I have occasional wee slip ups, as we all do. But I notice that, when I do, I don't seem to 'work' quite as well. I feel a little sluggish and my mind feels cloudy. Often, the best barometer of a healthy diet is how it makes you feel.

So given my own experience with life changes, I have found Carley's book compelling reading. While my changes merely made my body and mind feel better, Carley's may have saved her life. And she's not alone.

Whether people have noticed it or not, we're currently undergoing a kind of revolution in nutrition. A large number of medical schools, as of 2021-2022, are now incorporating compulsory courses in nutrition. The change is being driven by young doctors who have learned the benefits of lifestyle changes for themselves and frequently prescribe lifestyle change before a pill.

Perhaps, within a few years, more and more people visiting their doctor will be given lifestyle advice instead of medication, where it is appropriate. I am an optimist by nature. It is already happening, albeit only in small pockets here and there. A few of my friends are GPs and are part of this change. I believe it will become more widespread. The rapidly growing science showing the healthy benefits of particular nutritional choices, like plant-based diets, is compelling and impossible to ignore. It is also vital for our planet too, as plant-based diets have a very low carbon footprint.

I hope you take some inspiration from Carley's story. In these pages, she shares some of her life story and the challenges she faced, so you can have a context for the health situation she found herself in. Then she shares what she did about it, the changes she made to her mindset, lifestyle, and food intake.

Carley also has a fantastic sense of humour, and her light-hearted style shines through many of the pages of this book. I hope you enjoy the read and learn something valuable from it. I certainly did!

David R Hamilton PhD

Preface

There's nothing like a life-threatening diagnosis to put a little perspective on life, right? How true is the adage: we don't know what we have until it's gone? Or how about the one that says we never truly appreciate life until we're looking death straight in the face. Do I believe everything happens for a reason, or that in every adversity is an equal advantage? You better believe it and here's why.

Being paralysed will have you appreciating movement like you never have, losing your ability to string together a sentence creates a burning desire to express; and not being able to see, well that makes you grateful for even the greyest day. It's an awful shame that we don't automatically look at life through this brightly coloured lens, but hey I feel blessed that this has been my perspective since I was 23. Millions of us are given a life-altering diagnosis every day; for me, I was diagnosed with Multiple Sclerosis in 1999. Unable to move the right-hand side of my body, I couldn't stand, walk or even go to the toilet on my own. Unable to hold a lucid conversation, my words were jumbled, incomprehensible and when they eventually left my lips they were slurred and uncomfortable to hear. I can't even express how scary losing your sight is, because sometimes there just aren't the words. But this is where my miracle begins, aged 23, facing no cure, no cause, no real treatment and what felt like no hope.

The question is, how many of us millions choose how we interpret our diagnosis, our labels, our so-called limitations? How many of us take the official expectations of what life is going to be like and turn it on its head? Put a proverbial middle-finger up and say let me show you what you can do with that prognosis, that outlook, that expectation of my future. I'm hoping that after reading this book there are far more of us.

These pages are for those who are questioning their official diagnosis, challenging popular expectations and choosing to redefine their ability to take control of their health and wellbeing. I'm writing this book to speak directly to those who have the strength, courage
and conviction to take full responsibility for every aspect of their life, but primarily their health. I speak to those who have been told by everyone that they can't, but have chosen to say "just watch me".

We are the trailblazers, the boundary pushers, the new definers. Together, by sharing our stories, we are writing the future of medicine, of health and of just what our healing capabilities are. I'll be honest, I'm so excited just typing these words, sharing my story, telling you my why; because I know, because I didn't give up, because I decided to do things differently, because I reversed my diagnosis, you might do too. Anything is possible and we are quite literally limitless. My story shows how I am not my diagnosis and neither are you.

I decided to include some exercises and questions to work through in a journal at the end of each chapter, because I want this book to inspire you to put your health, your world, and your life into perspective. By working through these exercises, like me, you may begin to claim back your personal power and responsibility and feel good about doing it. Take your time and really dig deep into your thoughts when completing them and when you're finished, I'd love to hear your thoughts.

I've divided my journey into three themes, the first three chapters are about my diagnosis, how it was delivered, how I received that news and my reaction to it. The next two chapters are where I take an honest look back at my younger life and make some correlations between my behaviour, my environment and my childhood, and how they weakened my immune system and filled my body with inflammation. Yes, this is me saying that I have a timeline of events that lead to my diagnosis and that it wasn't random or just one of those unfortunate things. The last four chapters are where I begin to touch on the steps (leaps) I took to reverse my diagnosis. This section is not an in-depth, step-by-step, how-to and I have been intentional in this. Exactly what I did, and continue to do, on my Way to Wellness is a whole book in and of itself.

Chapter 1: What a difference a day can make

Day one: I woke up knowing that something wasn't quite right. I had pins and needles down the right hand side of my body, not just the regular pins and needles, you know, the ones you get when you've lain or sat funny. No, these bad boys were more like nuts and bolts running up and down my arm, torso, leg and face. I also couldn't seem to get the words out of my mouth the way I wanted to. Now I know that sounds bizarre. Trust me; the feeling was no less crazy. Have you ever forgotten what you were about to say mid-conversation, like you've lost your train of thought? Of course you have. Well that's not even close. Try to imagine that the words are there, on the tip of your tongue, you know exactly what you want to say, but they just won't come out. When my words eventually left my lips, they were slurred and uncomfortable to hear. So what did you do, I hear you ask? Nothing of course, I've been raised to get on with it! The show must always go on!

I was working two jobs at the time. I'd jump on a bus, get to my first job for 6am, cook breakfasts for a bunch of workmen; bacon and egg fry-up anyone? Not a great way to start your day, especially for a non-meat eater! Then it's off on a second bus journey, into University by 9am for a day of research and lectures, then back on another bus to my second job, bookkeeping; arriving home just before 7pm to look after my young family. Yes, I've always been a grafter, I was raised that way. Twelve to thirteen hour days has always been pretty standard for me so no amount of pins and needles, or nuts and bolts, was about to change that. On with the show!

Day two: Now the pins and needles have morphed into painful cramps. It feels like each one of my veins is being ripped out of my right side with tweezers, while my muscles, tendons and bones are fighting to keep them in. Painful doesn't even come close. My slurred words aren't getting any better either. Now my partner has begun to notice that something isn't quite right.

"Are you okay Carley? You seem a little strange this morning?"

With a glare I snapped, "Yes, I'm fine, just a little tired maybe."

Then yes, you guessed it, back to another twelve hour day, like the machine I was trained to be; more cooking, more studying, more bookkeeping and more being the dutiful housewife and mother.

Day three: My Mum is on the phone; my slurring must be so bad by this time that she asks me if I'm drunk!

"At 8am Mammy, not bloody likely!"

She immediately sprung into mother mode.

"Stay there, do not move, I'm on my way right now!"

Ten minutes later she took one look at me (I hadn't noticed the melting act my face had started to do by this time) and declared, "Oh my God Carley, I think you've had a stroke!"

A what? Don't be crazy I thought; but maybe there was something wrong, I was now numb down the right hand side of my body, I was dragging my leg when I walked, my face had melted and I couldn't speak properly. Yes okay, something definitely wasn't right, but a stroke, me, surely not? One very emotional ambulance ride later, with sirens and flashing lights to boot, I'm in hospital being told, "Yes Carley we believe you have had a stroke."

At twenty-three, are you lot crazy? That was my first thought, my second was, No fu**ing way! And my third, as I looked around the ward filled with elderly, very unwell people was, WHY?? Why me?? Why now??

I'll be honest; anger was my first emotional response. Anger because I'd worked so hard to get to where I was; working my way through university was my dream come true, I didn't have the time for this STROKE. And who the hell was going to pay my bills if I couldn't work? And that perfect little baby boy I had waiting for me at home, he needs his Mum whole, not half melted. I was bitter, angry and pissed off! I'd never felt so helpless, I was such a fiercely independent woman, to now be dependent on everyone for EVERYTHING; degrading doesn't even come close. Have you ever had to wait to be taken to the toilet, or to the shower, or to bed? Imagine, you can't even brush your teeth alone, because you can't get the top off the toothpaste; God we take so much for granted.

Confusion kicked in at this point, I was getting worse. The numbness was now full on paralysis. I had no control whatsoever over the right side of my body. I didn't recognise my face in the mirror or the jumbled words falling from my mouth and now I can see two of everything. What, am I going to lose my sight too? What the actual f**k? Two weeks of being pulled, prodded, and having my wee measured on the stroke ward, I'm told I haven't had a stroke after all.

"Your symptoms are getting worse Carley."

You don't friggin say!

"We're going to transfer you over to the neurology department at the Queens Medical Centre for further tests."

Send me where, for what? Now rage is kicking in, I am fuming that I have been treated as a stroke patient for all this time. Normally after a stroke you are left with a degree of damage which may or may not improve with time; very rarely do the symptoms continue to get worse. Yet, even though my symptoms had been getting worse by the day, it still took two weeks to figure out there was more going on.

So I'm in the Queen's Medical Centre floor D, I've had various neurological tests, invasive needles in my spine (lumber punctures are the worst) CAT scans, MRI scans, you name it, I had it. I began physio in my third week. I was able to sit up by then but had no control over my hand movements. I could wriggle my fingers - just - but there was no coordination. I had to do exercises with putty and a penny to regain my dexterity. Constantly squeezing and manipulating the putty, rolling it into shapes, pushing and pulling it, then picking up and putting down a penny; all with fingers that refused to do what my brain was willing them to do. I'd spent weeks telling myself, "I can do this! I will do this!" I wanted it now and it just wasn't happening quickly enough for me. That penny came to represent all my irritation and frustration. On more than one occasion I remember flinging it across the room in exasperation, but then of course, I couldn't actually get out of bed to pick the penny back up! The sheer frustration made me break down in tears. One day it happened when my mother-in-law was visiting. She walked in and caught me crying. I was always strong in front of everybody; I hated that she had seen me cry, because then I got the full sympathy routine, and I definitely didn't want sympathy.

I've just thrown my penny across the room in frustration, yet again, and my consultant walks in.

"Good morning Carley, I have some good news and some bad news. The good news is, there are no tumours on your brain, you do not have cancer. The bad news however, your scans have revealed a number of lesions. I'm afraid you have Multiple Sclerosis."

"Multiple Sclerosis? I've heard of it before, but what the hell is Multiple Sclerosis?"

"What I can tell you is this, there is no cure, and you may never recover. To date, we have yet to identify a cause, the treatment I have on offer for you today in not guaranteed, but really is your only hope at a somewhat normal life. My advice would be to quit University; the stress of studying will be far too great. Your health is going to be highly unstable from here on in and you may never get a job. Oh, and if I were you, I wouldn't have any more children. Any questions?"

Questions, not right now, no. You see I'm lying here, half the woman I was, I can't stand properly, I can't walk on my own, I can't even hold my son. My face looks like it's been in a liquidiser and I'm struggling to see; I've had three weeks of this, three weeks of poking , prodding and testing, for you to tell me there is no cause, no cure, no real treatment, and basically no hope. You have the audacity to advise me to quit University; you have no idea how hard I worked to gain entry. You tell me to prepare to never get a job, because I'm going to be 'too ill' from here on in. And to put the cherry on top, you tell me not to have any more children! Are you insane? (Okay my thoughts were a little bit stronger than that.)

Now I was really angry, how dare you tell me to expect the worst, to get ready for a life of illness; great outlook for a 23-year-old woman at the start of her adult journey. So I do what I do best when I don't hear what I want to hear, I search for an alternative voice, a different outlook, one that's based on more information, a better understanding and a brighter bloody future than he just painted for me.

I read about how my immune system has turned on itself, about how it's destroying my myelin sheath, my protector of the internal highway of neurological communication. I'm being attacked, to all intents and purposes, by my own defence system, but why? Million-dollar question it felt like at the time. With no answer from the trained professionals, looks like I'm going to have to answer this on my own.

"We're not sure of the cause Carley."

Oh right, so I'm meant to accept that it's just one of those things; that I just have to deal with it, right? WRONG! My gut told me not to listen to them and since my gut has never lied to me yet, I agreed with it and paid them no mind.

All around me people were telling me that this is how my life was going to be from now on, I had to make the most of it, to just accept it. I had almost reached that point of acceptance. It was because of that penny that I didn't. I used the frustration to say, "F**k them! I'm going to do this!" It was living through that frustration that pulled my determination back. With perseverance, I eventually began to get some control over my actions.

What about the medication I was being prescribed? For the first three weeks I was given intravenous steroid therapy to reduce the inflammation. This gave me the worst metallic taste in my mouth, a foul mood and a very hot head. I knew that this wasn't it. I had speech therapy, and was told at one point that I may never be able to talk normally again. Really, me, not talk? The idea was inconceivable.

"Can you tell me what the long term side effects of steroids use are? I've read about the gastric issues it causes, is this right?"

"Yes it is Carley, but that's why we give you stomach protection."

"OK, so I've read that steroids strip your body of calcium and other vital minerals, is this right?"

"Yes they can, but this is why we prescribe you calcium supplements."

"And what about the changes in my mood and my temperament, I've read…."

He interrupts me sharply and with little patience.

"Well Carley, I suggest you don't read any more; it's clearly upsetting you and not helping us treat you at all."

Well you can imagine what this spurred me on to do. Yes, read a whole lot more.

By the time I had my meeting with the consultant, I had enough doubt-filled questions to last him a lifetime, or that's how he made me feel. When I took out my sheet of A4 paper he rolled his eyes as though to say, here we go, they have told me about you.

"So Carley before you get lost in your curiosity, let me give you this piece of medical advice. Without beta interferon you may never walk again, your chances of going from relapsing and remitting to progressive Multiple Sclerosis is very high. It's my official opinion that you shouldn't refuse the medication on offer. Of course it's your choice, but I think it would be very irresponsible to do that. Just think of your son, your family, they need you. Without treatment your future doesn't look very bright."

"Okay, thank you for your opinion , before I make my decision can I just clarify," he rolled his eyes again, "whilst on this medical trial I'll have to have a liver function test and a kidney function test, is that right?"

"Yes that's correct."

"But there's nothing wrong with my kidney levels so presumably this medication is going to cause issues elsewhere in my body, is that right?"

"Well we have to monitor that as it is possible."

"And," I continued," it's probable that I'm going to feel like I've got the flu pretty much all of the time, is that right?"

"Again Carley, yes it is probable, but surely that's a better option than not being able to walk or talk?"

I think to myself, well I've had the flu before and I couldn't even lift my head from my pillow. Yes I can't walk right now, and yes my speech is slurred, but I sure don't feel like shit!

"Can I ask you about the results, how effective is this drug? You've given me a glimpse into the side effects but what is the success rate?"

"Well Carley, this is a very new treatment, it is cutting edge technology and the long range results are just not known yet, it's still very early days. But if you choose to let us help you, you'll have the very best monitoring and the very best care and you'll be helping so many other people with this condition. We need people like you to join the trial so we can monitor the benefits and the progress"

Or the deterioration and side-effects you mean?

"Sorry, I just need to clarify, the medication that you are offering me is not guaranteed to help in the long or the short term? You don't know what caused my condition, because, as of yet, you haven't identified one? Should I decide to take the pharmaceutical approach my other organs could become damaged and I may experience a range of life-dulling side effects, is that right?"

"Well, I wouldn't put it quite like that. Clearly you have to weigh up the potential benefits. Maybe your family can help you make the decision."

And maybe I'm capable of making my own, I thought to myself.

"I'm going to do some more reading and think about my options."

"Well don't wait too long Carley; your condition could get a lot worse."

Let me just get this out there from the outset, I have so much respect and admiration for our National Health Service. Without our medical practitioners, 1000s if not 1,000,000s of people would have undoubtedly died. Without them, or the initial treatment that I received, I may well have been in a wheelchair for months, my paralysis may have lingered for longer and my eyesight may not have returned. I believe that we are ALL very fortunate, here in the UK, to be able to get lifesaving treatment on the spot, regardless of your bank balance. I also think the nurses, doctors and auxiliary staff are undervalued, under acknowledged and most definitely underpaid, and the strain is showing, but I'll talk about the rate of burnout in GPs later in the book. However, do I want to be on medication for the rest of my life? Of course not. And did I feel confident putting my future into the hands of the medical professionals, who, by their own admission, didn't know much? Hell no! Was I irresponsible and stubborn? In the opinions of many maybe, yes I was, but my gut said keep the faith and I did.

Exercise: Visualisation

This first exercise I want to start you with is one that I use in my workshops. It's a powerful tool to help you put your life, your worries, and your stresses into perspective. We take millions of things for granted daily and often focus on and worry about insignificant things. This small visualisation exercise will help you to put whatever life is throwing at you into a more positive and hopeful context. When you have finished the exercise, give yourself at least five minutes to think, and write about the journal question. It's a huge question, so do it justice and don't skip it!

1) Think of an issue that is causing you major stress right now. Feel the emotion. Rate it on a scale of 1 to 10

2) Now imagine you have woken up paralysed.

3) Visualise all the things you can no longer do: dress yourself, eat, drive, work etc.

4) If this was your reality, what would you miss the most?

5) Now return to the major stress you rated earlier and re-rate it.

Funny when we put 'problems' into perspective they seem to melt in severity and importance.

Journal Question

If you only had 24 hours to live, who would you call, where would you go, what would you do?

Chapter 2: In the face of doubt

I don't know if you've ever been faced with a potential life or death decision before, but let me tell you there are a million and one reasons you should listen to everybody else's opinion. Unintentional blackmail is one of the hardest bags I've ever had to carry, and I say unintentional in the essence of pure love. Did my responsibility to everybody else outweigh my responsibility to myself? Did what I believed to be right, to be the right choice, make me totally irresponsible and selfish?

Pull on my heartstrings number one: I had a perfect six-month-old baby boy. I wanted to hold him but I couldn't. I wanted to run to him when he cried but I couldn't. I wanted to bathe him and feed him and do all the things that a young mother wants to do, but I couldn't. The paralysis down my right hand side meant I had to be handed my son if I wanted to hold him. Someone else had to tend to his tears because I couldn't walk to get to him. The fun of splashing and playing in the bath I could only listen to from the other room. Heartbroken doesn't even come close. And if I choose not to have a lifetime of medication I might never be able to do any of these things again.

Pull on my heartstrings number two: My partner, bless him, was now a carer. Not a role he'd signed up for but one he took on the best he could. He'd gone from having a fiercely independent, energetic, life of the party, no limit-living girlfriend to having two children to look after; his new six-month-old son and me. I couldn't do any of the automatic stuff for myself that we all take for granted. He bathed me, he took me to the toilet, he helped me brush my teeth. He combed my hair, he rubbed cream onto my skin, he dressed me. When I say this poor man became my 24-hour a day carer, I mean it. How then could I even think of refusing medication? My supposedly only chance at a somewhat normal life. Surely I owe it to him to take whatever they offer me?

Pull on my headstrings no 3: The doctors and nurses who had cared for me over the four weeks in hospital had helped me so much. Without those intravenous steroids my movement might never have come back. I could have been in that wheelchair even now. So clearly, Carley, I thought to myself, medication works. I couldn't deny that. My speech therapist who persevered with me, even though she told me I may never speak again properly - clearly she didn't know me! I'm so grateful for all of them. But then does my gratitude automatically mean that I'm indebted to them? To never question them, their advice or challenge their understanding or approach? It just didn't feel right. Despite the heart-pulling pressures, the nights of second guessing myself and trying to play my own devil's advocate, I just knew that was the wrong path for me. And yes as I actually said no thank you to the Beta interferon my head shouted to me, "Are you fricking crazy?" But my heart whispered, "They haven't seen crazy yet."

You see it's when the bullying started that I knew I'd made the right decision. No seriously, medical bullying is a thing. Have you ever questioned your doctor or told them you didn't agree? How dare you, you lesser, uneducated, child-like person, you? Ok, that wasn't their exact words, but that's certainly how it felt. Sherri Gordon[1] identified a number of signs of a medical bully, and let me tell you as soon as I declined my prescription I experienced ninety-per-cent of them. Refusing to answer questions was one of the first highlights. Although the consultants I dealt with didn't overtly refuse to answer me, there was always a marked distaste in their reply; especially if they didn't know the answer. Displaying arrogant and self-righteous behaviour? Tick. Speaking condescendingly? Tick. This was a regular occurrence with every repeat visit to the hospital. Unsurprisingly this still happens to this day. Not that I go to the hospital that often any more, but when I do I'm still treated like 'one of those' patients.

I can totally understand why so many people wouldn't go against the grain when making such a significant decision. The fear we are fed is constant and overwhelming. If you don't take the medication you may never walk again. If you refuse our advice you may go blind. Carley don't be so irresponsible. Don't you realise you could die from this?

This very bleak view of my future was played over and over and over again. I was bombarded with immune-lowering tales of fear and worry. I was even threatened with being taken off the medical register. Think about it, no more access to primary care should I need it in the future. Well, thanks for that. Now, I get that the majority of doctors just want to help. After all they've studied for years to be able to do just that. But to blatantly disregard informed and evidence-based conversations is quite frankly an insult.

Moshe Frenkel M.D., the founder and director of Integrative Oncology Consultants, hit the nail on the head when he pointed out in the journal The Oncologist that patients who refuse conventional treatments are self-

---

[1] Gordon, S. Is Your Healthcare Provider Bullying You During Appointments? 2019

directed, confident, active and have thought deeply about the meaning of life.[2]

I've said it before and I'll say it again, there's nothing like facing death to make you appreciate life. In my book quality will always outweigh quantity. Imagine, what if I wasn't as strong willed as I am? Imagine if the barrage of negative reinforcement of fear had succeeded? I honestly think I'm immune to the nocebo effect. Maybe because my inner placebo is so strong. No, seriously I think if we did an industry wide study of how patients are given diagnoses and prognoses by their doctors we'd get some really interesting results. Well actually no, it's not interesting, it's actually quite concerning. Being 'medically hexed' according to the founder of the Whole Health Medicine Institute, Dr Lissa Rankin, being pronounced with having a chronic or irreversible or terminal illness, doctors are actually programing our subconscious with negative beliefs, which actually activate stress responses.[3] And imagine what a major factor in multiple sclerosis is? Yes you've got it, stress. You know maybe if I'd been supported in my decision - no not encouraged, let's not take it too far - just supported on my road, maybe my reversal might have been a little easier or even speedier. But, then again I've learnt so much along the journey I wouldn't actually change any of it, even if I could. There's one thing for sure though, the effect of my words on my clients are at the forefront of my mind. As a healer my duty is to create a stress free environment in every and any way I can, and not fill my clients with fear and lack of connection.

I think this was one of the hardest decisions I've ever had to make and very much a life defining moment in so many ways for me. We are raised to place such trust and reliance on outside sources and such little on our own power and knowledge. From here on in, it was down to me. No one else to blame if it all goes wrong. Was I scared? Yeah, of course I was, but not as scared as I was of not taking responsibility, of not standing up and doing all that I could do to help myself. Do you know one day I'd like to do a mass survey and ask people if, when faced with a life or death decision, would they trust themselves? I think more people like me, the non-medically trained, would. I think they would and I think they are ready to stand in their own conviction.

---

[2] Frenkel, M. Refusing Treatment. Oncologist. 2013 May; 18(5): 634–636

[3] Rankin, L. Mind Over Medicine: Scientific Proof That You Can Heal Yourself. 2013 Hay House

Exercise: I am my only constant

This next exercise is designed to help you remember that you never let YOU down. I think we all too often forget just how strong we are, and rarely do we acknowledge, or dare I say celebrate, how many times in life that we have been our own hero. Here we are going to take an honest look at not only the strength that you may have forgotten you have, but also blocks in life that you may have allowed others to put in front of you.

1) Make a list of at least five issues in your life that you have faced alone.

2) Make a list of at least five times you have been let down by others.

3) Make a list of all the things you wanted to do but were told you couldn't.

4) Ask yourself did you survive and how?

Journal question

When was the last time you doubted yourself and stopped yourself from being / doing / saying what you really wanted to?

Chapter Three: Strength in my own conviction

This wasn't the first time I'd ignored all official advice, but my history of being stubborn wasn't always so successful. Dancing for example, was one of my only releases as a young girl. Yes I was overweight, yes I was under height, yes I was on points and in a tutu and yes it was my happy place. I remember wanting to get into the Christmas panto so badly. I'd auditioned unsuccessfully for two years on the trot but it didn't stop me from trying and trying again. So here I was 12-years old, lined up with all the other dancers. They were tall and slim, I was short and fat. They were being fussed over by their dance mums, I was on my own. They looked down on me, literally, whispering, "What is she doing here?" But I kept telling myself I could do this. I'd been practicing so hard, stretching for hours and doing time steps until my toes blistered. Yes, of course I was nervous, but once I got on that stage the comments, the looks, the doubt all disappeared. I did it, me, a little fat girl from the inner city. I was selected to be in the 'A' team.

I think this was another major seed in my disregard for what other people told me I could and could not do. Clearly if I believed in me and if I put the work in, I could achieve more than anyone ever thought I could. I danced my little heart out that year, all over Christmas, two performances a day for weeks. I was in heaven. The next year I auditioned again and bagged myself a place on the chorus line. My dream of becoming a professional dancer was another year closer. I could literally taste my equity card, it was so close.

You know when the universe has another idea and sends you lots of painful lessons of why this isn't going to be your future? I noticed that my knees began to swell and ache. But I was training so hard, that was normal right? Wrong. During rehearsals for Peter Pan my knees gave way. One wrong leap and bam, I fell horribly to the floor. Everyone around me gasped, they had heard it too. Turns out I had dislocated my kneecaps. That was painful but I think the shock took over. A little ice, maybe some rest, I'll be fine, I kept telling myself. I refused to give up dancing. I wore knee supports and strapped them every day. But now my knee caps would dislocate just by walking down the road or turning over in bed. I remember being in knee splints for six months. I couldn't climb stairs. I couldn't walk without crutches. But all I could think about was getting back on that stage. It was the only passion I'd ever had, the only goal I'd ever set for myself.

The only place I felt I belonged was on that stage.

And here I am sitting with a knee specialist who is telling me that if I don't give up dancing I'll end up in a wheelchair. And if I kept on I wouldn't even be walking let alone dancing. I didn't want to believe him but the pain I was in every minute of every day told me that he might have a point. Walking after all is slightly more important than being able to dance - I guess. But even then, instinctively, I knew I'd dance again. I didn't know where or how but I knew that dance would always be a part of my soul.

When I think about it, I've had a few of these moments growing up, when I've been told I couldn't or shouldn't do something. Thankfully, not all of them turned out to be quite so painful. My educational journey for example; I had lots of these moments peppered through it. Like when I decided that I was going to get myself into university, because working as a hairdresser was just not filling me with drive or excitement. I can remember one of my college tutors telling me that my writing style would never get me through university and that I was far too critical. I was trying to run before I'd learnt to walk - pun intended. Well maybe he was right but that comment fuelled my determination, yet again, to prove the doubters wrong.

"I am going to get into university," I told him, "and I'll get the highest grades possible."

"Good luck with that," he replied, flippantly.

That is exactly what I did. Ok, it took me five years to complete my Batchelor of Science but I was hell bent on finishing. And I did. I finished with one of the highest first class degrees of my year. And I won a couple of awards to boot. Despite being a young mum, despite having six monthly relapses, despite losing my sight at least once a year, despite the breakdown of my relationship with my partner, despite my Dad dying of cancer, despite all the challenges life threw at me, I never gave up. I remember walking across the graduation stage at Loughborough University with my head held so high; my family and friends in the audience. I'd done it! I'd achieved everything I set out to achieve.

I honestly think that most people run from personal responsibility because unwittingly or not we've had it taken from us from a very young age. Parents reluctantly take it from children; teachers blindly take it from students, and doctors, well they're taught to take it from their patients. I haven't decided yet whether it is the established institutions that take it away from us or that we willingly give it away. It's like we've been indoctrinated not only to accept giving up our personal responsibility but actually to be more comfortable with doing just that. Let's face it, it's easier to give our responsibility up, then there is always someone else to blame. The teachers, the politicians, the police, the doctors; we seem quite happy as a society to say to authority figures "Here's my life, it's in your hands, if you mess it up it's your fault not mine."

It's so easy, and I guess comforting, to be able to lay the blame at somebody else's feet. For some reason I was always ready and willing to take ownership of all of my choices and my actions from a really young age. Basically to stand in my own conviction. And do you know what, thank God I did.

There is quote by Eleanor Roosevelt, First lady of the United States between 1933 and 1945, which perfectly sums up my feelings: "You gain strength, courage and confidence by every experience in which you really stop to look fear in the face. You are able to say to yourself, 'I have lived through this horror. I can take the next thing that comes along.' You must do the thing you think you cannot do."[4]

---

[4] Roosevelt, E. You Learn by Living: Eleven Keys for a More Fulfilling Life. 2009. Westminster John Knox Press

Exercise: Celebrating Myself

The next exercise might prove to be the most uncomfortable one you undertake in this book. Why? Because we don't celebrate ourselves often enough. Boasting, showing off, or just congratulating yourself isn't the done thing in our society and is all too often frowned upon. In my opinion, we need to reintroduce self-celebration into our daily practise, and if you have children help them to become more self-assured adults by cheering their wins too.

1) For the next seven days spend two minutes (yes, you deserve two minutes) creating a self-appreciation break.

2) List all of your proudest moments

3) Celebrating yourself should be a daily practice, what did you achieve today that made you think 'well done me'?

Journal question

If you could give yourself any reward - no limits, anything your heart desires - what would it be and why?

Chapter Four: A wayward mind: Childhood programming

Okay, here's where we go back, into my unique childhood setting and the series of events that lead to where I stand today. Life as a mixed-race child was filled with imbalances, mismatches; let's just say it didn't quite fit. My Mum came from the Mellors family, one of the first travelling showground families from the 1920s. The Mellors family still run big shows such as the Goose Fair in Nottingham and the Big Wheel in Nottingham's Market Square. They run Winter Wonderlands and urban Summer Beaches around the country, as well as traditional fairgrounds in smaller parks. They had everything from sideshows to hot-dog stalls, candy-floss stalls to arcades; children's rides to hoop-la stalls.

The Traveller's life was all consuming. There was no going home at the end of the day and putting your feet up, there was always something else to do. You'd get up early, do your jobs, open the fair, graft all day, close down, eat supper, clean up, go to bed, get up and do it all over again. When it was time to move on, you'd pull everything down and pack it away, move on to the next site, set up and repeat the process all over again. This was the routine almost all year round. Once the Christmas lights switch-on was over, the fairgrounds stopped until Easter. During that shut-down we still didn't rest. The men repaired the rides or built new machines for the new season. The women would find work in local factories, anything to earn money to see their families through the winter. Some people did winter markets, my Mum did car-boot sales, while others had novelty shops. The work was constant.

My Mum raised me as a show woman; hard working, materially driven and a 'more is better' view of the world. Whereas my Dad, a very quiet, a very isolated, a very humble man, who although wasn't very overtly spiritual, lived a life of simple pleasures and pursuits. I don't know if you could find two opposing cultures with such different views of the world coming together like this, but let me tell you, as a product of this union it's not easy.

My Mum spoilt me; spoilt me because she felt sorry for me. Because my Dad wasn't overtly attentive or overtly loving, like her Dad had been, she literally gave me everything and more. I was covered head to toe in gold jewellery. I remember one of my nicknames outside of the fairground was

Mrs T, because I had so many chains and rings. This was pretty standard for the daughter of a show woman. She was so proud of me, her little creation. I remember her saying to me, "The only thing they can call you for babe, is your colour." Bless her. She did the best she could in the circumstances she'd chosen for herself and the challenges she faced because of it.

The life of a show family is magical. Well, it is for a child anyway. I had a fairy-tale childhood. Every day was different. I'd wake up to the sound of birds. I'd roam for hours in the fields, picking berries. I think that was one the most exciting things as a child, that every day was so different and exciting. Different parts of the country, different fields to play in, lots of different rides to play on. It was a sensory overload; the lights, the music, the adrenaline, the money, the glamour, the sugar, the fats. I'll be honest, I'm so glad we're not travelling anymore. Show people work hard; harder than hard. From the very youngest to the oldest, everyone has a role. You see, there is no division between work and home. The work is your life and your life is your work. There's no clocking off, there's no holiday, there's no sick pay. The show grounds were all there was, and that was that.

By choosing to have me, my Mum had walked away from all of that. Dating outsiders was taboo, in fact more than taboo. But by dating a black man, getting pregnant and having the baby, my Mum had broken every rule. She chose to leave a life of, what many could say was privilege, and the Mellors legacy, to live, work and forge a life in a very foreign world. Honestly, I don't think she ever recovered from losing her community and her place in it. After my Grandpa died when I was only six-months old, she was compelled by duty to return to the show life. She returned with her head held high, and with her perfect little chocolate drop baby in tow.

From Monday to Thursday my Mum and I lived in a house with my Dad, then we'd pack up and spend Friday to Sunday in a trailer on whatever showground the fair happened to be on that week. Once the family realised my Dad wasn't just a passing fancy they allowed him to help out. He would occasionally help my Mum at the big events like Goose Fair, but he had his own 9-5 job, so it didn't happen very often. Also, while they were prepared to accept his help, they weren't very welcoming. It can't have been a very pleasurable experience for him.

As a very young girl I had lots of friends on the show grounds. I don't think the overt prejudice struck me until I was about seven, or maybe I just blocked it out before then, for the sake of my own sanity. I remember being at Buxton Fair when I was about seven or eight. I love Buxton Fair. I went to call on one of my friends who I had played with every year up to then. I got to the wagon, knocked on the door, and while I stood outside I could hear all my friends inside laughing and giggling.

"Shhh, don't open the door!" I heard one of them say.

I was confused and embarrassed. I must have stood there for about ten minutes expecting them to open the door at any moment and let me in. But they didn't.

On other occasions, it was the parents of my friends who would tell them to leave me on the footboard because they didn't want me inside their wagon.

I've even heard comments such as "Come here, let me lick your lips and stick you to the window."

Now as an adult I know this was all learnt behaviour. They had learnt it from their parents and their parents had learnt it from theirs, and so on back through the generations. This is the way they treated people who were different from them. And boy was I different! The ONLY black child on the fairground ever.

I didn't have a choice about whether to go to the show grounds or not. But even if I did I wouldn't have chosen to stay at home. You see, as painful as the racially prejudiced comments were, I loved this business. I loved the buzz of the fair when it was open. I loved setting out, getting the hotdogs ready and beautifully presented; I loved dipping apples, bagging candy and even cutting bread, although peeling bags of onions I could have done without. But yes, I loved it all. I smiled with the punters and I sold my little heart out. When I think about the business skills I learnt at this stage and how they have been ingrained in me, there's no wonder I'm a self-employed business woman today. Yes the behaviour of the travellers, their words and their ignorance hurt and stripped away at my self-confidence. But as quickly as they stripped away I'd have to say that I rebuilt. I learnt very quickly that other peoples' opinions of me didn't count and didn't reflect my opinion of myself. Well, mostly. When I look back at some of the defence mechanisms that I adopted I can see clearly the effect the overt prejudice had on me.

Yes, I turned to food, and later on in this book I'll tell you a little bit more about the processed fats and the sugars that I turned to, that I leant on, and how that affected me in later life. But for now, picture this. I was 10 stone at age 10. I became so overweight that we couldn't buy clothes from ordinary shops. Fortunately both my Nana and my Mum were tailoresses. I spent a lot of time with my Nana as a young girl. I have to say that she was, and still is, my style icon. She was Hollywood glamour personified; always pristine, her hair, her nails, her clothes. She had the most elegant ankles. I know that is a crazy thing to remember about your Nana, but they really were striking. She'd wear 1940's style pin-stripe skirts that came to mid-calf, which emphasised her ankles even more. I would watch her manner for hours and just wish I could be more like her. She was slender and petite where I was round and swollen. I would sit and compare my legs to hers and wonder why I wasn't more like her. I remember thinking; I hope I have ankles like that one day. Despite looking like a pudding back them, today I do indeed have my Nana's shapely ankles!

I remember feeling her disappointment in my Mum and in myself. Her daughter had brought a 'black' cloud over the family. It wasn't until I was older that I found out that the cloud wasn't just about my Mum.

I was raised by the strongest women I know. My Mum and my Nana did it all; they ran the business without a man. When my Grandpa died, they took over his role, driving the lorries, coupling the trailers, building up the fairground machines. They minded the candy-floss stalls, they built up the stalls, and they pulled them down and all of the jobs in between. I am so grateful for the foundation they both laid for me. Truly, I wouldn't be the woman I am today without them. When I think about it, much of my 'I can do anything' mind-set and attitude is due to both of them equally. My trailblazing, my rule bending - or breaking - was from my Mum. My style, my presentation was from my Nana. As painful and as challenging being raised on the show grounds was, I wouldn't change it even if I could.

Was it easier or any less painful being at home? Nope, it sure wasn't. There was always an air of tension at home, like the two lifestyles didn't quite meld, but no one ever dealt with it. My Dad was born and raised in Jamaica. One of 10 children, he didn't come to England until later in his teens, and then he didn't want to come at all. In fact he spent most of his working life making enough money so he could travel back home to Jamaica three or four times a year.

Now discipline, that was the theme from my Dad; strict doesn't even come close to describing what he was. I remember my Dad not wanting, or allowing, me to do anything other than go to school; even sleepovers were outlawed. Can you imagine going from what I perceived to be a prison from Monday to Thursday to being let loose into this world of freedom and exploration at the weekend? Well, that was my world until I was 16. One incident I remember very well was being grounded for six whole months. When I say grounded, it wasn't like grounding is for some children, who could still watch television and speak to their friends on the phone. No, my six months of grounding meant school, home and my bedroom. Friends would come to call and my Dad would close the door. They would call on the landline asking to speak to me and he would put the phone down on them. I wasn't even allowed to go to the shop. It must have been something really bad that I'd done to deserve such a harsh punishment, I hear you thinking. In my Dad's eyes it was. You see, I had a curfew, 7pm on the dot. On this particular occasion I was five minutes late. Yes, you heard it right, five whole minutes! I was held hostage for six months because I came home at 7.05pm. Harsh? I thought so then. In fact I remember feeling hatred towards him. I planned to run away so many times but I was scared he would find me and lock me up forever. So I did my entire six months begrudgingly and filled with resentment. Friends who knew him called him 'Superman', not for his love of humanity and his deeds to save the world, but for his death stare. My Dad had eyes that could burn the very soul from your body without a second thought.

He was a very quiet man, unlike my Mum who was very loud. He was silent and in a state of contemplation most of the time. He was not motivated by material possessions, again unlike my Mum. He didn't strive for the finer things in life. His music, his love for Jamaica and his spliff seemed to be his only drive in life.

So here I am, a young girl filled with material ambitions of glamour, covered in gold, filled with feminist ideas that I could do it without a man, living with a Dad who disapproved of, or at least that was how it felt, everything the Travelling world stood for. A perfect recipe for rebellion if ever you saw one. He hated every ethic my Mum had taught me. Apart from keeping our house like a show home. Cleaning, now that was one skill that fitted into his world of structure and discipline.

I was 12 when my Dad stopped talking to me. I can hear you saying "How can a Dad stop talking to his twelve year old daughter and still live under the same roof?" A question, I can assure you, I asked myself for many years. I actually understand it now though, honestly I do. We had an in-depth conversation about this, and many other things, on his deathbed. But at the time, this lack of communication with my Dad just fuelled an already bitter and acidic and contentious view of the man I now referred to as Mr Blair. I used to write him hate letters and leave them on the side of his bed. I can only imagine how painful it was for him to find and read these letters; but he never showed any emotion anyway, so what did it matter?

Oh how I rebelled! I climbed out of my bedroom window to escape. I started smoking. I went to parties I shouldn't have been anywhere near. The gold jewellery - signposts around my neck and on my fingers - attracted boys

- men - and generally not very nice ones. I did everything I could, and more, to cross his line. And I didn't look back. I cut my all hair off and died it gold. Yes, ironic I know. I began to dress more like a gangster than a princess. Baggy shorts, bandanas, big stomping boots, to walk the streets of Nottingham, which I often did at all times of day and night.

Now school and studying, that was something I also rebelled at. I barely went. In my last two years of school I had the belief that the subjects they were teaching held no interest for me and they definitely didn't have an impact. Many teachers tried to help but some didn't. There was one teacher in particular, oh how I made her life a living hell. She was already a very nervous woman, and then along comes Carley making her the target of all my frustrations. I became the class disrupter and if I'm honest I probably made her dread coming to work, or at the very least, dread teaching history to any class I was in. Ironically, history turned out to be one of my favourite subjects later in life.

Almost 16 and my Dad had decided he wasn't going to put up with my antics or my attitude any longer. My Mum had lost all control of her perfect little chocolate drop, and he kicked me out. 16 and homeless, filled with anger, rage and a warrant disregard for all authority, or figures of discipline. I sofa surfed for almost two years. Blessed with friends who would again help me to learn some of the most valuable lessons in life: survival. Lessons that would never leave me.

There were six of us altogether, bad breeds some would say. Products of our environment, I like to think; lost souls just looking for somewhere to belong. I felt at home with these girls like I never had before. Even though I'd clearly had a privileged childhood that some of them never had, they took me in, taught me how to cope and called me sister. I'll never forget any of them. Things could have turned out so differently without them in my life.

When I look back it was such a dark period. I had no money, no home, no stability. I literally had to steal to feed and clothe myself. I once stole a chicken, concealing it under a long skirt, waddling out of the shop with it clenched between my thighs. The art of survival I acquired during that time couldn't have been learnt any other way. Yes, I'm calling it an art, because that's what it was, a skill that I became adept at. I was involved in activity then that was, let's just say south of the law, but when you need to survive, literally it is by any means necessary.

Do I regret any of it? No, not at all. I wouldn't be the survivor I am today without that time. But I can say now that karma, or the law of increasing returns, kicked my ass for at least the next five years. Trust me when I say I paid for, and paid back, all the wrong that I did and everything that I had taken.

Blame? I could have blamed my Dad for making me homeless. I could have blamed my Mum for exposing me to constant and overt prejudice. I could have blamed the world for the lack of connection, the loneliness, the frustration and the anger. To be honest, at the time I did. It was everyone else's fault. He did it, she did it, they did it. Always looking outward for the source of our pain is a state I think we can all relate to. Thankfully, it was a state that was about to change. At 18 I noticed that some the girls I had been hanging around with had begun getting arrested, being sent to prison. I knew that life wasn't for me. I was lucky enough to be taken into a homeless shelter for women of colour. That was a pivotal point. It had been two years of craziness but I had got it out of my system. It was time to move on.

One of my very first earth angels, and I've had many over the years, saved my life by giving me a book. 'Nile Valley Contributions to Civilization: Exploding the Myths'.[5] And boy, did it explode my myths! I spent the next two years in splendid literary isolation.

---

[5] Browder, A. T. Nile Valley Contributions to Civilization, Exploding the Myths: vol one. 1992. Institute of Karmic Guidance

Exercise: I forgive you

This next exercise is yet another powerful, though potentially painful one. Forgiveness is a huge part of healing, because we can't truly heal while we carry hate, anger, resentment, blame or distain for another human being. No matter what the circumstances, until you release and forgive you will always be filled with negative energy and the harmful chemicals that come with these emotions. Ironically you only hurt yourself by holding onto them, so it's time to let go for your own health and peace of mind.

This task my take longer than you think to complete, be gentle with yourself and take as much time as you need and repeat as many times as you must, until you feel the lightness of forgiveness flows through you. Our parents often repeat the same lessons or patterns that they themselves learned as children. They too can be operating from a wounded space. Parents can only parent from their own level of awareness.

1) Write a forgiveness letter to the child version of your Mum or Dad, or both.

2) Connect with their pain, their experience, their wounds.

3) Recognise that many of our childhood wounds have been passed down from unprocessed wounds that our parents have dealt with.

Journal question

Who is the one person you know you should forgive and what has stopped you up until now?

Chapter Five: An unconditioned body: toxic relationships

Now my mind-set was definitely strong but my body, not so much so. I've already painted the short, fat, outcast picture of myself for you, but my toxic food attachments really were the hard habits I had to break. Nobody taught me - nobody teaches us - the fact that we literally are what we eat. So yet again, here's another universal law that I had to learn the hard way. So many people, young and old, use food as a comfort tool, as a go to; that one thing that we can control. It's ironic, because as most of us that overeat were ultimately controlled by the very things we put into our mouths. But here's the thing. I lived with 24-hour access to the very foods that most people only get to eat a couple of times a year: hot dogs, beef burgers, candy floss, toffee apples, brandy snaps and chocolate coated nougat. These things weren't just a treat for me. I literally had them on tap, anytime I wanted. It makes me cringe just thinking back to what I used to eat.

Parents, if your child is overweight, it's your responsibility to teach them, to show them, to help them not to be. Trust me, it's not fun being the fat kid. Children are honest and cruel. I don't care that you think that they might be able to cope with the bullying, trust me; the scars of being fat never go away. Funny story, can you remember Dynasty? Yes the shoulder pad wearing, big hair sporting, 80s TV show about the warring wealthy. Well, I used to go to bed and pray to wake up like Sammy Jo. Seriously she was my idol; blonde hair, blue eyes and all. I kid you not, I actually used to go to bed early so I could spend an extra half hour visualising myself in her body. Slim, didn't need to wear a bra, had legs that didn't rub together at the top, and arms that weren't the same size as most of my friend's thighs. I guess in a way this early practice of visualisation, of where I wanted to be and how I wanted my life to be, was great practice for the visualisation work that I now do every day. I didn't know how powerful it was, or is; but then it seemed another way that my higher self was using to guide me to use my superpowers to change my reality.

Seriously though, childhood obesity is one of the most serious public health challenges today. If current trends continue, over 70 million children will be obese by 2025.[6] I can personally testify that this group of researchers definitely show and are right that weight gain in adolescence leads to depression, poor self- esteem and anxiety.

Being bullied and teased for being overweight only made me eat more. I know: oxymoron. But the power of control that I felt by being able to eat whatever I wanted, whenever I wanted, seemed to somehow soothe the lack of control that I felt in every other aspect of my world. I wasn't black, but I definitely wasn't white. I couldn't control or do anything about that. Thanks Mum, thanks Dad!

I wasn't poor. I didn't know any other kid who was poor, who was covered in gold like I was, but I definitely wasn't rich. Well, not according to my Mum, as she constantly complained about how much money we didn't have. I wasn't a traveller; well not a true traveller. How could I be? My skin was different, I lived part time in a house and I went to school all the time. But then I wasn't a joskin (a non-showman, or an outsider) either. Confused.com!

What I was, what I could rely on, the only thing that was constant in my world was my weight. I was fat. Ok, clearly there are some emotional scars that come with being a disconnected girl who was very obese. But when I look back, the physical ailments, the screams that my immune system was making, were definitely loud. It's a shame that nobody recognised the signs earlier. For example, I remember having mouth ulcers from really young, I mean six or seven. My nana used to say "Oh, my babe, I've never known anybody so young to have mouth ulcers like you have." As she dabbed Frador onto my gums. I don't know if you've ever rubbed Frador onto mouth ulcers, but it's like rubbing acid on an open wound. Let's just say, it bloody hurts.

Now there are all sorts of horrible causes for mouth ulcers in children, but a weak immune system is right up there. But compared to having glandular fever every year for five years, mouth ulcers were a walk in the park. Yep, you've got it, another painful cry for help from my immune system. Glandular fever not once, not twice, but every year, like clockwork, for five years. In fact, the memory of that is still so vivid that three decades later I can still feel how scared I was to swallow my own spit. If you've ever had glandular fever, you'll know exactly what I mean. There is so much

---

[6] Rankin, L. Mind Over Medicine: Scientific Proof That You Can Heal Yourself. 2013 Hay House

research now into the link between glandular fever, also known as the Epstein Barr virus, and MS But hey, it wasn't a thing back then.

Wait, there's more. My body was trying so desperately to talk to me, well, to anyone who'd listen. Problem is, we've never learnt the language. How about having chicken pox, not once, not twice, but three times. Anyone who believes that you can only have chicken pox once is very misguided. Again, another viral infection that can linger in your system for years. Thankfully I've not had resurgence as an adult as shingles but then my constant cellular cleansing takes care of all that kind of possibility.

According to the Medical Medium, Anthony William, all these symptoms I experienced were variations of the Epstein Barr virus. My eventual diagnosis of MS was just the virus in its fourth stage of development. I remember reading this: "the medical communities believe there is no resolution for multiple sclerosis. They are mistaken."[7] I remember thinking, finally, someone who gets it. Someone who gets that the so-called incurable can be cured and not just put into remission.

Anthony William, suggests that "the only hope of killing your Epstein Barr virus is a strong and vibrant immune system" Ironically, most medications prescribed to treat MS do exactly the opposite, these medications are designed to weaken and suppress the immune system and not bolster and strengthen it. So not only are these drugs failing to help you defeat EBV, they're significantly aiding the virus" This was even more confirmation of what I already knew, that these immune suppressing medications I was offered by the hospital was, in my opinion, the wrong thing to do. It is not the way to deal with MS. I didn't need to weaken my natural defences to stop my body attacking itself, I needed to build it, to make it stronger. I needed to build my immune system so it could defeat this, and any other invader that tried to get into my system.

I learned that high doses of vitamin C, intravenously administered is one of the only reported ways to kill this virus. I'm sure as science progresses and we better understand our ability to heal, we'll find even more ways of ridding our bodies' potential invaders like this one, but for now, finding a source of IV vitamin C was on my radar. It's crazy to think that these 'natural' methods aren't offered more widely, or even common knowledge among professionals who treat people with autoimmune disorders. Why is it that

[7] William, A. Medical Medium: Secrets behind chronic and mystery illness & how to finally heal. 2015. Hay House

individuals like me have to take it upon ourselves to hunt research and find these methods alone?

With my diet of processed fats and sugars, my immune system was in a constant mode of defence, and I had effectively eaten my way into the perfect biological storm. When I look back, not once was my diet ever suggested as a factor to my condition, but I know this was another area I had to address, again not that I had to weaken my immune system, but I had to stop triggering it by the food stuffs that I was consuming. Letting "food be thy medicine" isn't exactly a new concept, is it? Why then is most doctors' knowledge of nutrition so rudimentary? In 2020 a report published in the British Medical Journal, highlighted that 85% of doctors felt their nutritional training was inadequate. And get this, 70% reported only two hours of training on the importance of nutrition, which equated to only one module across a five-year degree.[8] A slight short fall wouldn't you agree?

Now I'm not taking away from personal responsibility here, I'm not suggesting that it is solely the responsibility of doctors to teach us how we should eat for optimum health. But I am suggesting that if more doctors were versed in nutrition, they wouldn't need to be so heavily reliant on chemical answers to lifestyle problems. If our plate and what we put onto it can cause so many issues, then surely we should start our quest with that very plate? As the strains on our National Health Service continues to increase, coupled with the financial haemorrhaging, and the rates of burn-out our medical staff, I'd argue that a life-style approach must take centre stage.

You see on so many levels, emotionally, nutritionally, environmentally, physiologically, my system was under pressure. If I was going to achieve the impossible it's on all of these levels I had to heal, not just one, but all of them. Not an easy task, I hear you say. No, it wasn't. I knew it would take everything I had, but I was ready. I was willing, I was able, maybe stubborn, but I knew I could do this. I had to do this. My life wasn't going to be this.

---

[8] Macaninch, E. Et al. Time for nutrition in medical education. 2020. British Medical Journal.

Exercise: Nutritional intake

I've included the next exercise to help you take a good look at your nutritional intake. What is it you're putting on your plate and feeding your cells every day? Most of us eat for taste, for the pleasure of food and I'm not saying that's totally a bad thing, it's not, we should enjoy our food. However, when it comes to healing and staying health, nutritional content must play a major role too.

Take the next seven days to really get to know and understand what it is that you eat. What vitamins and minerals you give your body and why our bodies need them to function effectively. This was an eye-opener of an exercise for both my clients and myself, so be ready to be shocked, educated and motivated to make a change.

1) Keep a food diary for one week. No cheating, no judgement, this exercise is just for clarity.

2) Review your nutritional intake

We are what we eat. Much of what we eat is unconscious. We don't always eat because we are hungry. We often eat for comfort.

Food Diary

	Breakfast	Lunch	Dinner	Snacks
Monday				
Tuesday				
Wednesday				
Thursday				
Friday				
Saturday				
Sunday				

Journal questions

1) What does food mean to you?

2) If you only made one change to your diet to improve it, what would it be?

3) Do just that!

Chapter Six: Reshaping my body: a nutritional journey

The first time I realised just how powerful what we eat and drink can be was when I was prescribed Methotrexate. I collected the prescription from the chemist, who advised me to wear gloves to take the tablet. Well, you can imagine my face. Gloves? What the hell? I've got to swallow this drug, why do I need gloves on just to touch it.

I sat down and read the information leaflet inside the packet. To my shock and horror I'd just been prescribed a chemotherapy drug, with no consultation, no explanation, not even the consideration of letting me know. To this day I am still dumbfounded how doctors can prescribe this type of medication without letting their patients know exactly what it is. So of course I didn't take it.

At this point everything else had calmed down but I was still haemorrhaging behind my optic nerve, which meant the steroids clearly weren't working. I'd been told without the Methotrexate it could turn cancerous. I needed to find a natural alternative. I needed to find a cytotoxic source that wasn't going to attack every other cell in my body.

My research took me on a mind-blowing journey into the cancer industry. Yes, I did mean to call it an industry, but that subject alone could fill a book in its own right. So I'll stay focused and just include the findings relevant to my diagnosis and my replacement, or a natural alternative, to Methotrexate.

Soursop, also known as Brazilian paw-paw or graviola, is a fruit native to the south Americas, Caribbean Islands, Africa and Southeast Asia. The bark, leaves, root and fruits of the graviola tree are widely used by people in these countries to treat viruses and parasites, as well as rheumatism, arthritis, depression, and sickness. It is known to have cytotoxic properties, be extremely high in antioxidants, to fight bacteria, reduce inflammation, lower blood sugar levels and help prevent heart disease. I was on to a winner!

One of my friends told me that her mother-in-law had been diagnosed with breast cancer some ten years ago and friends recommended she drink the tea three times a day for at least six months, and the cancer had been treated. Miracle treatment? Well, no. It has been researched and known about for many decades, but again it hasn't been publicised. I could say a lot more about this, but no, I am going to resist the urge to go too deep.

So I decided that I had to find the leaves and the bark by any means possible. If I had to jump on a plane and go to Jamaica, I'd do just that. It turns out my Aunt in Jamaica has a tree in her back yard, so all I had to do was go and collect the leaves, pick the bark and I was sorted. Thankfully, one of my uncles was out in Jamaica at the time and brought me back bundles of the leaves and bark. I did a bit more research and realised it was sold in Jamaican shops right here in the UK, so I didn't even need to rely on him after that.

Well, here I go, boiling the leaves and bark and drinking the tea three times a day as instructed. Not a great taste, but hey, I didn't need gloves to handle it, so win-win in my book! My family and friends would quiz me on what the hell I was drinking. A witch's brew, I used to joke. But many a true word is said in jest.

I had my next follow up appointment with the consultant six weeks later. We already had a love-hate relationship. He'd been prescribing me steroids since I was first diagnosed 12 years earlier, and we'd have heated debates at each annual consultation, about steroid therapy and my approach to multiple sclerosis. Basically, every time he prescribed something chemical, I'd try to find an alternative. It actually says on my medical notes 'self-medicates with herbs.'

I decided not to tell him what I'd been doing. I'd let the test results do the talking first. Then I'd drop the bombshell.

"Well Carley," he said, peering at the test results. "It looks like the Methotrexate has been working. The bleeding has stopped and the inflammation has been reduced significantly."

"Really!" I replied, wanting to get up and do a celebration dance. "That's interesting, as I've not actually been taking it."

There was an uncomfortable moment of silence, and then a look of horror spread across his face.

I smirked and asked, "Have you ever heard of the soursop tree and its cytotoxic properties?"

"You mean you've been drinking bush tea?" he replied in such a condescending tone. "No I haven't heard of it."

I was stunned. He was a very prestigious African doctor who was head in his field, yet he was being so totally dismissive of it. I went immediately into defensive mode. Surely if this 'bush tea' has had such an amazing result, without all of the side effects and without costing the NHS a penny, I would have thought a more enthusiastic response was likely, or at least he could be a just a little inquisitive. But no, all I got from him was total disregard.

Hey, I thought, it isn't the first time he's brushed you off, don't take it to heart.

Every time I saw him after that he asked if I was still on the bush tea.

"Yes, I am," I told him, "and it's working."

Using our diet as medicine isn't a new concept. Hippocrates, a Greek physician, said "Let thy food be thy medicine and medicine be thy food"[9] as long ago as 400BC. But to me it was a whole new world of discovery.

Here I was, aged 37, I'd recently left my husband, with two young sons in tow, around five stone overweight, much of which was down to the overuse of steroid therapy, and I felt like I was just at the beginning of my healing journey.

I had what I thought was a healthy diet. I'd stopped eating red meat and pork many years ago. Not for any health reasons, I just didn't like it. I had always eaten lots of fruit and vegetables; I was raised that way by both my parents. My Mum was brought up on 'proper' dinners, meat and two veg, which she continued with me. My Dad was a pescatarian. His traditional Jamaican diet consisted of hard foods, vegetables such as yams, banana, plantain and fish. Nothing was pre-packaged, store bought, everything was cooked fresh. But this new revelation that if drinking the leaves and bark of a tree could stop the bleeding behind my optic nerve, what else could food do?

By this stage I had already decided that I no longer had Multiple Sclerosis. After all I hadn't had a relapse for a number of years and I hadn't been to the MS clinic for nine. But this inflammation around my eyes was like the last man standing; my final test of faith and will. I decided that food was going to be my weapon of choice. I'd read that fasting was a great way of reducing inflammation in our bodies so I decided that was where I'd start.

I'd never fasted before so I thought that maybe a juice fast might be an easier way to start than to attempt a total water fast. I bought two books by Jason Vale, a motivational speaker and lifestyle coach; '7lbs in 7 days: Juice Master Diet' and 'The Juice Master: Turbo-charge Your Life in 14 Days.' I then bought myself what I thought was a very expensive juicer, but I am still using it now, many years later, so it definitely paid for itself.

I set the date, bought the ingredients and mentally prepared myself not to use my teeth for seven whole days. My youngest son had his second birthday that week and I entertained and cooked for 30 members of my family. Yes, all whilst fasting! Was I tempted to break the fast? No, not at all. In fact the challenge fuelled me even further. Of course, my family thought I was crazy. All this beautiful, delicious food and there I was drinking green, swamp juice.

---

[9] Science Direct: European Journal of Pharmacology. 2018 October; 836: 102-114

Mmm tasty!

Now, I'm not crazy. I promised myself if I experienced any extreme detox effects I'd stop. I was far too busy at work and had to run a home single handed, so I couldn't afford to be stuck with withdrawal symptoms. I also employed a personal trainer to help push my exercise to the next level. Yes, by now you know that I don't do things by halves. If I'm in, I'm in all the way.

To my amazement and to my personal trainer's astonishment, by day three I had more energy than she knew what to do with. I was out-reping her to the point that she asked me what the book was called and what plan I was following, because she wanted to do it too. Let me tell you, by the end of day seven I was not only nine pounds lighter in excess weight, but I felt more energized than I ever had before. It was like every cell in my body had been supercharged by life. If I could feel like this in only seven days, what else could I achieve?

My first solid meal was an explosion of taste and colour; every vegetable you can think of - except Brussels sprouts, I really don't like Brussels sprouts. I'd never had such an appreciation for food, for taste, or for using my teeth before. I think it took me nearly an hour to eat my first meal, and I was so full afterwards. I actually only ate one meal a day for the next week, as I was so in love with my juices and smoothies, I couldn't stop having them.

My next stop was what Jason Vale called the 'seven deadly dietary sins'.[10] I'd taken so much of what I ate out of my diet that I didn't want to just put it all back. So I started with milk. I'd never really liked milk. I'm sure many of you of a certain age will remember those little bottles of milk with an inch of cream on the top that we had to drink at school, and how disgusting they tasted, especially when they'd been sitting in the sun for hours beforehand. I remember projectile vomiting at nursery because I was forced to drink the stuff. After I'd read this chapter of Jason's book, I understood why I had always instinctively disliked it. I'd been raised, like many of us, to think of dairy, milk and cheese as a very good source of calcium. But when I dug deeper, I was shocked by the misinformation and lies we've all been fed for generations and generations. Vale tells us that we are the only mammals on the planet to drink milk after weaning. When you think about it not even cows drink milk, only calves do. And more apparent, we are the only species

---

[10] Vale, J. 7lbs in 7 days: Juice Master Diet. 2014. Harper Thorsons

to drink the milk of a totally different species. It's like common sense, but then common sense isn't always that common.

It was what he said, however, about the protein casein that gave me all I needed to know. The base ingredient of superglue is casein. The main protein in milk is casein. That means, every time you drink milk you are basically covering your digestive system, your entire digestive tract, in superglue. Well, no wonder the absorption rate of our nutrients is so low. I decided then and there that I was never putting milk back into my diet. I took cheese out, I took cream out, well to be honest I never really liked cream anyway. I have to say that sometimes I still eat dark chocolate, but since I learnt how to make my own with coconut oil and cacao and a little agave syrup to sweeten it, it isn't that often at all.

My eldest son didn't like the changes I was bringing into our kitchen, but I didn't give him much choice. My Mum started calling me anti-social because she couldn't even have a cup of tea when she came to visit. I'd just laugh and say, "Mum, I'm saving our lives, one drink at a time."

Besides, there were plenty of teas in my cupboard now, nettle, dandelion, milk thistle, ginger, lemon; all fresh, all loose, and not a teabag in sight. It's crazy once you stop to think about what we put in our mouths and realise just how much we don't know. But as Donny Miller, an author and motivational speaker, put it, 'in an age of information ignorance is a choice.'[11]

Shopping trips at first became a two-hour exploration. I went over every label with a fine toothcomb. Let's be honest, half of the stuff listed on the packaging we've never heard of, can't even pronounce, and have no idea what it does. I wonder when we actually became so complacent about pre-packaged food that we stopped even bothering to read the labels. I'll be honest, I felt like Alice, fully down the rabbit hole. At first sugar, sweeteners, wheat, pesticides, sulphates, parabens; what the hell was - is - the food industry doing to us? The more I learnt, the more I realised I didn't know. How on earth can we be fed so much chemically laden food, or non-food stuff, as I like to call them now? It should be criminal, but it isn't.

Next, I cut out bread, which I have to admit, was much harder to do than milk. I was a total bread head. As I learnt more about simple carbs, their low micronutrient content, I felt so much lighter by taking them out. It literally

---

[11] Miller, D. Beautiful People with beautiful feelings. 2006. Abrams Image

became the proof in the pudding. Breaded goods are such a staple part of most peoples' diet. Toast for breakfast, sandwiches for lunch, I think many of us eat between four to six slices of bread a day, every day. The more you eat, the more you want, right? It wasn't until I started reading about how bread can spike your blood sugar levels, which can cause you to actually eat more, that it really hit home. Have you ever eaten a hearty breakfast of cereal and toast, believing it to be healthy, and then been ravenous an hour later? Well, do some more digging. There's a scientific reason behind it.

My kitchen began to look more like an apothecary by the day; jars of herbs, nuts, seeds, pulses. Much to my son's disappointment the biscuits, the crisps and the sweet treats disappeared. As did the sauces, the spreads and the dips that had been on our shelves for years. Why do we as parents convince ourselves that treats should be sweet? Sugar filled goodies are, in the words of Jason Vale, 'more dangerous to our health than any other product.'[12] He says they are 'the cocaine of the food industry.' I was called mean by so many people for cutting out this nutrition-less, highly addictive, disease-causing rubbish from our diets. Did I care? Of course not. My liver, adrenal glands and other vital organs were celebrating my choices. And that's all that mattered.

Within six months I had lost even more weight. I had even more energy. My skin was glowing, my eyes were bright and my brain was bursting with ideas; so many, so fast it was hard for my pen to keep up. The thing is when you feel this new energy, this zest for life you just want to share it with the world. I wanted, and still want, everyone to feel as good as I was feeling. So many of my clients and friends kept asking me if I was still on that juice diet. They'd pull a face at the sight of my bright green juices. They may have looked disgusting, but they tasted like Heaven. I'd laugh to myself and tell them: "It isn't a diet, it's a lifestyle. There's no going back to 'normal' Why would there be?"

People would comment on how good I was looking. They'd ask how was it possible that I looked younger now than I did ten years ago. "It's no secret," I'd reply. Then I'd start telling them about the massive changes I'd made to my eating habits. With shock and horror on their faces they'd say, "What, no bread? No milk? No sugar? Surely, no life. No, Carley that sounds like hell. I couldn't do it."

---

[12] Vale, J. 7lbs in 7 days: Juice Master Diet. 2014. Harper Thorsons

It amuses me to this day how many people want to feel and look healthy but don't want to make the changes in their life to achieve it. Yes, it's hard at first. No, it isn't a sprint or an overnight jump, it takes effort and discipline; being consistent and dedicated. Being healthy doesn't come automatically. But over the months, over the years, it becomes like autopilot. I don't have to put the effort in anymore like I used to because now it's my way of life. I don't use packets of food, I don't have jars of sauces, I don't have frozen food in my freezer, I don't use a microwave for my convenience, but I have the vitality of a toddler. The motivation and the drive and the stamina and the health of any world class athlete. Were the short-term sacrifices worth my long-term gains? You better believe it!

I eat to live; I don't live to eat. Is my diet dull, unvaried, or any less tasty? No, not at all. In fact I think there is more variety, more colour and taste in my food choices now than there ever has been. I totally agree with Dr Michael Greger, an American physician, author, and professional speaker on public health issues, when he says: "We almost eat as if the future doesn't matter."[13]

Well, guess what? My future matters, and it's bright and sparkly at that.

---

[13] Greger. M. Dr. How Not to Die. 2017. Pan Macmillian

Exercise: Fasting, an introduction, taking a digestive break

Okay, our next exercise might be another little challenge for you, but I've got faith in you! Choose a day that you can be still, be calm and only intake water for 24 hours. Don't panic, at least eight of the 24 hours you'll be sleeping anyway, but if you're still having heart palpitations at just the thought of not using your teeth for a whole day, then take baby steps. Try 16 hours first and when you see how easy that was, then move up to 24. Honestly this is more of a mental challenge than a physical one, trust me your body can cope for a day without having to digest food.

Digestion is by far the most taxing process our bodies must go through, since we rarely give it the time off, the break that it so desperately needs. Your cells will thank you on the other side. The energy and light feelings that you eventually get once fasting is a part of your health routine are astounding. Did you know that after 72 hours of water fasting your body generates new immune cells? Yes you read that right, three days of just water and your body starts to make brand new stem cells for you.[14]

Fasting - baby steps

1) Prepare yourself mentally and try a 24-hour water fast challenge

[14] Cheng C. et al. Prolonged fasting reduces IGF-1/PKA to promote hematopoietic-stem-cell-based regeneration and reverse immunosuppression. 2014.

2) Write down how you feel and what fasting does to and for your body

3) Take a digestive break at least once a month.

Journal questions

1) If I were my ideal shape, what would it look like?

2) Why am not there already?

Chapter Seven: Reconnecting my soul: following my joy

To heal emotionally, my joy, my happiness, my peace of mind and my excitement for the future had to be my priority. There are so many studies about how health is affected by our emotional state and although the traditional take is always focusing on the negative emotions and how they can harm, there's a growing body of research that looks at how happiness can heal. If happiness makes our heart healthier, our immune systems stronger and our lives longer.[15] I have to make a massive move to connect to my joy. Now, for me to be truly happy I have to have peace of mind and there's one huge part of my world that was filled with anger, resentment and frustration. Yep, my relationship with my Dad, or more to the point, my lack of one. I made a massive decision at that point to face my fear. I know that sounds crazy, because he was my Dad, but you already know he was a scary man. Now confessions, would I have done this if he wasn't on his deathbed? Would I have been so brave if he hadn't just received a terminal diagnosis? Would I have done it if this wasn't my last chance to reconcile with him? If I'm honest, probably not. My first thought wasn't really for him and how he was coping with this cancer news. No, my first thought was all about me; he can't die before I get a chance to actually offload on him. Selfish? Yeah, I guess so, but come on this man stopped talking to me when I was 12-years old. I had a lot of pain he needed to hear and it was now or maybe never.

So there I was, scared to death, sweating my top lip off, underneath the mask and the plastic coverings and the plastic aprons, I literally felt like I was going to pass out. I was ready - not. I peeped through the small window of his hospital room and just looked at him, lying there in an oxygen tent, so vulnerable, helpless and less than half the man he used to be. My heart began to melt, and all that blame, all that hurt, all the resentment I wanted to lay at his dying feet, began to fall away. Don't get me wrong, he was still going to get it, just not right now.

I opened the door slightly and asked if I could come in. He looked at me, gave me the cut-eye, a visual gesture communicating displeasure, disapproval, or general rejection of the person at whom it is directed. Other than that he

[15] Newman, K. Six Ways Happiness is Good For Your Health. 2015

didn't respond, so of course I took that as a yes. I walked in and sat there, still sweating, not saying a word. It was just like when we lived at home, no talking, no eye contact, no connection. I kept having these flashbacks to all the times that he'd broken my poor little heart. Father daughter relationships, they're meant to be magical, right? Well not in this case, there was no bloody fairy tale here that was for sure.

So an hour passes and my time is up. No conversation, no emotional downloads, and definitely no release took place. But there had been a shift, a shift in my mind-set of how I viewed this man, my Dad. And just like that the start of an 18-month connection was made. Not only for him but also for me. I became one of his main carers from that day on. I got to offload, he got to offload and the bond that we formed before he died rendered everything that had gone before then irrelevant. What started out as a very selfish quest to get answers, ended up being one the most selfless acts that I could have ever given myself, or my Dad. I know that he crossed over to the spirit world a lighter version of himself. His estranged daughter who he disowned all those years ago wasn't quite as lost as he'd thought. In fact, he actually admitted that I was more like him than he ever thought was possible. We laughed, we joked, we ate, and we watched old black and white movies, and often we just sat in silence. When his time was up I had no more questions. I had no unresolved issues, no regrets, no blame, no heavy heart. Through my selfless act we both found forgiveness.

This example of reconnecting my soul didn't start off joy-filled, I know, but it certainly developed into one. And that peace of mind I found continues to fill me with joy to this day.

A systematic review of the biological factors of health and happiness by Dariush Farhud, Professor of Medical and Clinical Genetics[16] commented that health factors are critical in underlying happiness. So, as far as I could see, if I flipped that, if I made myself happy in every aspect of my life, then I could restore my health. From then on, I made it a priority that my levels of dopamine, my levels of serotonin, my oxytocin and my endorphins, all remained high and that stress-filled chemicals were kept low. Multiple Sclerosis or any other condition didn't stand a chance.

Ok, so that was happiness and peace of mind sorted, but what about my excitement, my drive, my thirst for the future? Now be honest, how often do you get excited? No seriously, as an adult is it not an everyday thing? Should it be an everyday thing, or am I just being optimistic? You know that

---

[16] Farhud, D., Malmir, M., Khananmad, M. Health & Happiness: The Biological Factors. 2014.

excitement you had when you were a child, when everything was a reason to be delighted. In fact you didn't always need a reason; even a smile could get you bursting with joy. Well, that's the kind of excitement I needed to reignite. Can't be that hard as an adult, surely?

I wanted to do things that made my heart beat faster. Life on the edge, I think I called it. Maybe more like irresponsible, according to other people. But that hasn't stopped me yet and it's not about to stop me now. So, I decided to quit a very secure job in politics and start my own holistic health business. Did I mention that during an academic break from Uni, I landed a job as a Constituency Assistant, and then got myself promoted to a Parliamentary Assistant to a Member of Parliament in the space of 18-months? No, well that's another one of those Carley challenges that I like to do, just because I can. Seriously, my eyesight was so bad on the day of my interview I went with an eye-patch on! Can you imagine? Thank you to Alan Simpson (then MP) for seeing my potential, regardless of my present health challenges, I'll be forever grateful for the opportunity you gave me.

Yes, I know it sounds crazy, but I did it, I went from working for a Member of Parliament to handing out Vista Print cards in local gyms and offices trying to convince people to book in with me. Now I didn't fully understand it at the time, why I was drawn to this therapy stuff, but it felt like it was a calling, one that I couldn't ignore. My family and my friends thought I was insane, walking away from a job that was literally my everything. It was what I'd worked so hard at university to do, political journalism. Now when I say I worked hard at university, what I mean is that I spent five years impressing myself, rising to every literary challenge my tutors presented me with, becoming a straight 'A' student and fully immersing myself into geek-mode! Yes, it was exciting, yes I loved every minute of it, but politics and becoming a journalist was yesterday's dream, and it didn't light my fire like healing did. Let's face it I was born to be a business woman. It was like a duck to water.

So I made another promise to myself, that my joy, my happiness, my peace of mind and my zest for life, from now on would be my GPS, my internal compass. If it didn't feel right, it was because it wasn't right. Now I have to admit, it took some time for this to kick in constantly. I had to second guess myself and question myself before this GPS became auto pilot, before I truly trusted it, but sure enough, over time, the layers of guilt passed away; guilt for prioritising my own passion, my own peace and my own soul's plan.

Exercise: My happy place: 60 second challenge

This exercise is another one of my powerful tools that I like to share at my workshops. This is another one that is all about YOU, your story, your passion, your happy place. Give yourself just 60 seconds every day to visit and play in your happy place.

Tip: This one works really well first thing in the morning, use it to frame your day with happy thoughts and positive energy.

1) Think of a place where you feel happy / safe.

2) Visualise yourself in your happy place. Stay there for 60 seconds. Set a clock. Yes, you are worth one whole minute!

3) For the next week go to your happy place for at least 60 seconds each day

4) List 10 ways that you find fun: do you sing, dance, draw, bake? What is your definition of play?

Journal questions

1) What stops you having more fun in life?

2) What is your favourite game and why?

Chapter Eight: Reprogramming my mind; upgrading the software

I love this quote from Napoleon Hill: "Whatever the mind can conceive and believe it can achieve."[17] And wasn't Mr Hill bang on the money? I had belief that I could beat multiple sclerosis from the outset and I did. I conceived of having the healthiest lifestyle ever and ok I'm still working towards that, but I did. What else could my mind achieve? I mean what other aspects of my world could I manifest miracles in if I put my mind to it, and kept it on it? I know it sounds simplistic, too easy, that "you can change what you are, where you are simply by changing your mind".[18] But, you've got to admit, my journey so far has been a living example of just that. Ok it's not been an easy road, but as Jim Rohn says, "don't wish it were easier, wish you were better".[19] So that became my driving force to keep going. A decade of hard work, blood, sweat and yes, lots of tears. But now I'm symptom free. More than that, I have more energy than I ever had, more drive than I ever had and get this; I'm feeling younger by the day. Why would I go back? Revert to my old ways of eating and thinking and being and doing? No not likely.

Now staying on track is what most of us find challenging. Let's be honest, discipline is a muscle that needs work like any other, if not it goes flabby. What's my motivation? How do I stay on track? I get asked this all the time. Well you remember that day when I threw that penny across the room because I couldn't move my fingers to pick it up? Or the time I had to ask to be taken to the toilet? Well that's my motivation; those memories, they are like almost ten years' worth, they keep me so motivated. They are still so vivid in my mind and my emotions, that I don't think that I'll ever be so complacent with my health again. But I knew there was so much more to learn.

In fact I totally agree with Socrates that "The only true wisdom is in

---

[17] Hill, N. & Clement Stone, W. Success Through a Positive Mental Attitude. 1959. HarperCollins Publishers

[18] Ziglar, Z. See You At The Top. 2002. Magna Publishing

[19] Rohn, J. Leading An Inspired Life. 1997. Success Partners Holding Co

knowing you know nothing."[20] And all those years later I still feel that the more I learn the less I know.

I turned myself into a virtual apprentice and worked with many virtual teachers, from Napoleon Hill to Jim Rowan to Earl Nightingale to Lisa Nichols to Les Brown from Anthony Williams to Dr Dispenza, from Greg Braden to Dr Lipton from Rob Sharma and Eric Thomson from Esther Hicks to Mel Robbins, I mean there are too many to mention. Talk about standing on the shoulders of giants, more like I've been feeding off the brains of gods.

After ten years in business and building a very stable clientele, I knew that I could do more, that I could reach higher, touch more people and share my story with as many people as I possibly could. If you've not guessed it yet, I get a little bit bored, quite easily, so I've always got to have the next challenge ready to go after I get through with the one, I'm working on. It has been said that this trait represents somebody with a high intelligence or maybe it's just down to me being raised on a forever changing fairground. Whichever it is, it's like a thirst for the new, a thirst that is never quenched.

Time for a change. I'd recently qualified as a nutritional therapist and began offering added services helping clients find out how their diet was affecting their health and wellbeing. I have to say it is so encouraging how education on diet and gut health has become much more widely understood today. Though I still have so many clients, including GPs and nurses, who worryingly know very little on just how important what we eat really is. Honestly, if I see another type-2 diabetic client who has been advised by their diabetic nurse that they can drink as much sugar-free pop as they want, I think I'll explode! Considering that Hippocrates, the father of western medicine stated that all disease begins in the gut and that we should let our food be thy medicine, how far has the mainstream medical industry really lost track?

From there I decided to add life coaching and purpose finding into my tool bag. Again as a functional therapist I knew that true healing depended on physical, emotional and spiritual connections. If it worked for me I had to be able to offer that to my clients. I had to encompass all these aspects in my approaches and found the most profound shifts when we connected to the emotional and the spiritual. But when I took my clients out of their everyday routine into a world of endless possibilities this is where the magic

[20] Goalcast: famous quotes from Socrates on life, knowledge and wisdom.

happened. And so Nature's Pharmacy International Retreats was born. I love to heal, I love to help people and I love to travel; why didn't I think of this before? Another strand, another branch to my ever expanding tree. My first retreat was sold out in less than a week. I know. Well I didn't make a profit; the price was ridiculously cheap, but then making a profit didn't come into it, it has never been about making money for me, well not as a primary motive anyway. But the experience, the knowledge and the difference I made to my guests on that very first retreat - that was priceless. Now I get that that sounds insane. And of course as a woman in business I am here to make money, but it's just never been my why. Probably why I have only ever increased my prices in clinic three times over 15 years. My accountant questioned me over and over again. I remember one of my business mentors advising me to double my prices and I would half my clientele but increase my time. Sound business advice I know, but if money was all that this was about I probably would have done it in a flash. But it wasn't then and it still isn't now.

Helping people being in service, helping those that need me, regardless of their demographic, regardless of their bank balance, that's my reward. I know that if I continue to render greater service than that for which I am paid, the law of increased returns will always work in my favour. That, if you didn't recognise it, is another one of the secret laws of success that I've kind of borrowed from Mr Napoleon Hill. But this ethos has always felt right so I have always used it. If selling out all of my events without having to really market them is the delayed payment or reward, then long may it continue, I say.

My clinic is so busy I often have a three month waiting list. I run three to four wellbeing retreats a year. I have a growing number of corporate clients who enlist me, my skills and my team to run wellbeing events for their staff. And still there's more I want to achieve. More? I can hear you say. Well, if you were a client of mine you already know this is not surprising. If this is our first tango, our first rodeo, then you're kind of getting the idea that 'more' is not only my motto, but my mantra. After all, growth is our purpose, right?

Now this phrase will always play loud in my mind, courtesy of one of my real-life teachers Oyi Son, from Atlanta, USA. How did I end up with an American mentor? Well clearly the student was ready and the teacher appeared. I remember he was the first one to push me out of my comfort zone, I mean completely out of it. I was so used to doing this on my own. This man taught me more about practical magic - also known as using the laws of nature - than I ever knew existed. I promised myself that if I could hit my target within a month I'd sign up with him for six months in his platinum coaching plan. I not only reached my target, cracked my goals, I completely blew it out of the water. So I signed up. I put myself right back into student mode. He was my first real coach but not my last. Over the years I've worked with business advisors, spiritual teachers, personal trainers, writing mentors, public-speaking coaches, and currently a world-renowned brand building powerhouse of a woman!

Here's a question for you, when did you stop learning? Why do so many see learning as being age and time dependent? It blows my mind. How many stop being students? I know it's not for everyone, even though it should be. I'll be a lifelong student. I owe it to myself and to all the people I help and will help, to keep pushing and expanding my levels of understanding, and most importantly to be a living example of the healing potential our bodies actually have. It's no longer about just healing my body or embracing my brain, my experience has shown me we can actually biohack our bodies, we can alter our DNA and we can achieve anything. This is why I say I know we are born to heal.

If you've made it this far through the book I know this idea isn't too woo-woo for you now. I know there are a few of you out there who can feel that you were born to heal. You know that feeling in the pit of your stomach that you can heal, overcome, thrive and grow through all that you are experiencing right now, I know this because you found this book and this book found you.

Exercise: self-analysis

Okay, it's about you again. This time your challenge, if you choose to accept it, is all about self-analysis. No, please don't use this as a time to beat up on yourself; I just want you to look how you could improve a little every day. That's really all it takes you know, just a small step every day in the right direction can lead to a life-changing journey. Be honest, who doesn't want to be better tomorrow than they were yesterday?

I think the greatest work we can do is on ourselves and thank goodness it's a lifelong task. It might be a new concept for you right now, but try being a student again, get all teachable and open to learn new things. Go find someone who has done things, achieved things you'd like to achieve, and learn from them. Remember you're never too old and it's never too late.

1) List at least 10 ways you can improve yourself daily, the small and the not so small.

Journal Question

When is the last time you did something for the first time?

Chapter Nine: Living my purpose on purpose

Purpose - now there's a word with weight; a concept and a calling. I have to be honest; I think my purpose has changed so many times throughout my 45 years and I honestly think that is a part of our evolution. I used to think that I was born to dance, and then I was born to be a journalist, and then a businesswoman and a health facilitator; and now? Now I feel my purpose is pulling me towards sharing my story, telling my why as far and as wide as I can: a published author, a public speaker, raising the awareness and understanding of our ability to heal. There are so many amazing testimonies across the world of people who have achieved miracles with their health. I am going to share a few of them from my clinic in a moment.

Over the last ten years the growth and acknowledgement of our ability to heal has been beautiful to watch. More and more people are standing up and taking full control of their health and wellbeing; whether it be physical, emotional or spiritual. My clinic is like a microcosm of this massive shift that is happening throughout the world; helping people to help themselves. I'm gratefully in service to the health and wellbeing of other people, and this it brings me joy, excitement, wonder and drive.

Now are all of my ways to wellness for everyone? No, of course not. Health isn't a one size fits all, how could it be? We are all unique. Just because these ways to wellness worked for me and most of my clients, doesn't automatically mean they will work for you. But - and it's a huge but - if this book has resonated with you, if you are still with me, nine chapters in, I'd say it has touched some part of you, then those methods can help you too.

First I'd like you to meet George, a retired transport director and the author of a series of children's books. His daughter had watched one of my Facebook videos and emailed me to see if I could help her Dad. George was very determined to get up and walk again, something he'd been told he'd probably never do. He was a very proud man but totally dependent on his family and his team of carers for everything. Well, after six months of intense work, not only for himself but for his team of carers too, George achieved amazing results. We didn't manage to climb his stairs like he'd originally wanted to, but I'll let his words tell you of his pride.

"I was diagnosed with MS some ten years ago. It has affected my mobility and to a lesser extent my memory. Several months ago I'd reached a real low level, ending in hospitalization for several weeks. With the consequence on discharge that I was virtually unable to stand, let alone walk. My daughter had put me in touch with Carley who had advised me on a clean diet and a regime of exercise. Both of which Carley monitored when she visited. The impact of the lifestyle changes has been to restore my increasingly limited walking ability from almost nothing to an ability to stand and walk using crutches between my rooms. I'm aware of an improvement in my physical strength and as a by-product, a reduction in my weight. The results of these changes are considered extremely positive, not just by me but also those close to me. For myself, Carley's approach has required a reasonable compliance to her dietary and growing exercise regime. Ultimately I recognised that only I could achieve my goal, but I am convinced that my progress so far has been hugely helped by Carley's invaluable guidance, encouragement and commitment. George."

It's amazing what a little accountability, some clarity and consistent action can do for our health. Even when we've been told there's nothing more that can be done. Here's another example of just how far we can come when we adopt a functional approach to altering our health. Let me introduce you to Andrea, she's a full-time facilities manager who yet again resonated with one of my online videos. Here's what she had to say about working with me.

"I followed Carley on Facebook, watching her live streams and listening, wondering what she would be able to do to help me on my journey. I watched and listened for a few weeks and understood and felt what she was talking about. I felt her passion and thought, yep, she can help me, and help me she did. I decided to sign up for a five week 'Reset' course to see how she could support me on my health and ended up signing for four more courses. Over this period of time we talked, we laughed, I cried; we covered many areas of life that you forget even make an impact. She gave me great advice and support, pulled me out of my comfort zone and had me on a path of sorting my shit out. She listened to me, she rapped my knuckles, and pulled me so hard it was crazy, but it was the best thing I ever did. That investment in me and who I am now was worth it tenfold and I will be forever grateful. If you are on a journey too, to find who you are, where you are, and where you want to be, or just simply need her to help you to 'sort your shit out', she's definitely a force to be reckoned with. Taking the plunge to be enlightened by a woman who has a spirit that I've not seen in anyone for a very long time. Carley, with your help and guidance, you've helped me and I appreciate all that you've done and continue to do for me. Andrea."

You know, it's funny; it's often when people are at their lowest that somehow the Universe leads them to me. Not that I have a problem with that, being the last resort, honest. No actually, it works in my favour, because that's when people have tried everything and yet they're still trying. They've been let down by every medical professional but they are still looking at ways to help themselves. That is my ideal client. Seriously, they're not quitters. They have a burning desire, and with that burning desire they can achieve anything. Speaking of non-quitters with a burning desire, meet Kimmi, she's a 37-year-old mother of two, who was born with a congenital heart defect and a whole host of other physical and emotional challenges. Her story is literally one of blind faith in the belief in the impossible. Here's what she had to say:

"I first started working with Carley when I had reached the lowest dip in my life. I was consumed by grief, by pain and by illness. The journey has been considerably hard but it certainly could not have happened without the help of Carley. Her holistic approach not only helped put me into remission from a very rare disorder, she has also helped me build my confidence. At the age of 37 I am now completing my dream of going to university. I have not been the most desirable patient, with many hurdles along the way, but not once has she allowed me to slip. She has been my confidante, that person that sometimes we all need to answer to. The devotion she has shown me throughout this process, and continues to do so, is invaluable. The opening statement when meeting Carley I will always remember, we must make you better for you first, then everybody else can come afterwards, because without you being the best version of you, you are not able to give people the best version of you. This statement I now live by and I will never be that parent that my children have to worry about. I will be the survivor. Thank you Carley, for believing in me. Kimmi"

Do you know what I really love, when the changes that I help people make indirectly and directly affects their whole family. Meet Paul and Gillian. Their story shows just how profound this kind of shift can be.

"We first visited Carley for help with my husband Paul who had suffered from chronic back and leg pain since spinal surgery ten years previously. He had been told that he had exhausted everything Western medicine could offer in terms of pain relief. It was a locum doctor who suggested cupping therapy, and so we turned up for an appointment with Carley. What a relief to find someone who actually listened rather than hearing the first few words and then making their own mind up; someone who didn't tell Paul, no the pain can't go from your foot up, when it actually did. Our lives changed for the better from our very first visit. We changed our diet; Paul was able to from down from 11 painkillers a day to just one at night. He came off his statins and his cholesterol reduced to normal levels. Even though the reason for seeing Carley was to help Paul, because we made all the changes together, my own health improved. So much so, that I retrained as a nutritional therapist. We have both adopted a far better and more natural lifestyle since that first appointment. Was it easy? No, not at all. Was it worth it? Yes, absolutely. Thank you, Carley. Gillian and Paul."

The amount of people that visit me who have been told there is no more that can be done, is heart-breaking. I mean, seriously, if you are a medical professional reading this, please stop that! Maybe there's nothing left in your tool bag but there's always more that can be done.

When these official decisions affect the quality of life of our children it not only breaks my heart, but it boils my blood. Meet little Athena. She came to my clinic in 2018; she was in pain, very uncomfortable and extremely sore. Her scalp was cracked and bleeding, to the point that her eyes were so swollen and crusted with eczema and her little hands were chapped and peeling. Her mum instinctively knew she had an intolerance to dairy, but she was made to feel like an absolute irresponsible mother when she suggested taking her daughter off milk. Well, after an intolerance test with me and some major changes to the entire family's diet, I'm pleased to report that little Athena's hair is growing beautifully, her skin is no longer bleeding, and she is the happy and pain free little girl that she should be. Her mum was understandably so angry at the doctors but so relieved that she'd taken the matter into her own hands. I am definitely all for putting the right fuel into our bodies and the proof is here with Athena.

"If we hadn't come to see you Carley, I think Athena would still be very, very poorly. It really doesn't put my trust in the GPs so a big thank you, to you. Athena's mum, Emily."

Unnecessary suffering that so many go through because the medical industry doesn't recognise the role of diet on our health, is ludicrous. Just think how much money health specialists and functional health specialists like myself, could save the medical system, if these methods were the first port of call.

Meet Lisa Jane, a young mother at the end of her tether, having been poked and prodded and treated and tested from her teenage years. It left her with no answer, and unlike me, almost no hope.

"I went to see Carley after what I thought was a severe reaction to food, but the doctors refused to test. Instead they told me to rip my carpets up as it was probably an allergy to dogs. I had a history of attending GPs with recurring UTIs, kidney infections and IBS flare-ups, with no explanation. After one session with Carley, after having my food intolerance test, I had so many answers to my original question. I am now in better health than I have ever been. I am feeling more energetic, have less sensitivity in my skin, no eczema flare-ups, and I've lost two stone in weight. I've got no more kidney problems or IBS issues. Carley, your guidance and support has made me 'me' again, and I know I can always access your support. I am so glad that I followed through on friends' recommendations to come and see you, or I don't know where I would have been now. Thank you so much, you have been so helpful. Lisa Jane"

Clearly changing your nutritional intake can have life changing effects, regardless of your medical condition. I think that this is a universally applicable tool; eat better, feel better. Great foundation from which to heal but then from my own experience and those of my clients, the emotional healing needed, that's where the underlying hard work lies.

Let me introduce you to Danielle, a young mother who has lived through most mothers' nightmare, a child being diagnosed with stage-four cancer. Her friends and family had raised some funds for her so she could come and see me for a couple of months. Let me tell you, it took almost 12 months for this lady to muster up the courage to come to my clinic. But once we'd started, the shift in her paradigm was nothing less than magic. I'll let her tell her story herself.

"I went to see Carley for help, feeling like I had some trauma and negative habits that I couldn't get rid of. A lot of childhood trauma I hadn't properly addressed, a toxic relationship I was trying to let go of, and my son was diagnosed with cancer. It was all consuming my mind, affecting my confidence and my quality of life. When I first went to Carley I just didn't know what to expect. I was nervous, but when I entered her beautiful room I automatically felt safe and welcomed. Speaking to Carley was so unbelievably easy. She offers a space where I could just express myself and it was unreal how much better I instantly felt. Being able to verbalise my emotions helped me to realise how much hurt and self-blame I'd been festering for many years. We focused on rebalancing my chakras, my energy centres, and reflexology, and oh my goodness does this lady have skills! I enjoyed the homework task that she set. OK some of them were a little bit hard and often left me in tears, but afterwards so much more than relief. They helped me focus and completely shift my consciousness to a whole new perspective. I no longer see myself as a victim but as a victor. I am so very grateful for the work this wonderful lady has done to help me. I am a better person thanks to such an inspirational and wonderful soul. Danielle."

I literally have thousands of these personal accounts of how people have decided, have chosen, to take responsibility for their health and wellbeing, physically, emotionally and spiritually. The story that I will close these testimonies with is of a woman who's journey mimics mine so closely. She is like a sister to me, not just a client. She's like most of the people who grace my clinic with their trust; she has become a member of my family. Meet Charlene, who after being advised to come and see me by people who neither of us knew, came wanting help to avoid medication to improve her MS. This is her story in her own words.

"Little did I know she would completely change my life in so many ways. Carley has helped me mentally, physically and spiritually. She is an absolute inspirational leader, caregiver and friend. I wouldn't be where I am now without her support, her guidance and I can't thank you enough. Charlene."

Not only did we improve Charlene's pain levels, her fatigue, her mobility and her zest for life, her brain scans actually showed marked improvements. She even had another beautiful baby girl, which both her and her partner had thought would never happen.

These stories, these lives, these recoveries are why I do what I do on purpose and with passion. Now you can understand why I say receiving this diagnosis all those years ago was one of the best things that ever happened to me. Although I work to prove that prognosis was wrong, without it, my life would have taken a completely different trajectory. Well, you wouldn't have been reading this book, that's for sure. Two decades later I'm still learning just how miraculous our bodies are. Two decades on I'm still pushing myself to keep growing and never taking for granted the trillion - 400 trillion - reasons that I have to be grateful. As I close this, my first book, I want to say thank you to all of the people who have made my healing journey what it is. I look forward to meeting the millions of people who are to be touched by my vortex. By no means does any of this book claim to be the answer to all health issues. Nor do I suggest that it will work for everyone like it has worked for me. But I do hope that I've shown you that you are not helpless, that there is so much more that can be done. That you can actually take responsibility for your health and wellbeing and begin to functionally approach whatever it is that you might be facing.

As amazing as the medical industry is, and as astounding as the chemical and surgical advances that we have made are, there is so much more to our physical health than reductionist mechanics.

I bring this story to you of my journey and my why to stand testimony that I am not my diagnosis. And get this, neither are you.

Exercise: Flight planning, the importance of goals

So we have come to our last exercise and what better way to close than by setting some dreams, some goals, and some objectives. Since you've completed every exercise in this book - which I hope you have - you have so many new ideas about what you want from life, what lights you up and what fills you with joy. Just by writing them down you set a whole process of activation off, and your dreams will be one step closer to you than ever before.

Take the time to ask what you really want to order from your life, if money were no object, if time, obligations, responsibilities had no bearing on what you can have, what would life look like for you? Do your future self a huge favour, set some goals and go get them!

1) List five short term goals

2) What resources do you need to achieve these goals?

3) Set a weekly/monthly schedule of tasks you need to complete

4) Reward yourself when you hit a checkpoint

5) List five long term goals

6) Repeat steps two to four

Journal question

1) What does legacy mean to you, what difference are you making?

2) What will people say about you after you die?

Bibliography

Books and journals

- Bowles, J. Why There is No Multiple Sclerosis at the Equator: How Brazilian Doctors are curing MS with high doses of Vitamin D3. 2013 CreateSpace Independent Publishing Platform
- Browder, A. T. Nile Valley Contributions to Civilization, Exploding the Myths: vol one. 1992. Institute of Karmic Guidance
- Frenkel, M. Refusing Treatment. Oncologist. 2013 May; 18(5): 634–636
- Greger. M. Dr. How Not to Die. 2017. Pan Macmillian
- Hill, N. Think and Grow Rich. 1937. The Ralston Society.
- Hippocrates: Science Direct: European Journal of Pharmacology. 2018 October; 836: 102-114
- Jelinek, G. MD Overcoming Multiple Sclerosis: The evidence based 7 step recovery programme. 2016 Allen & Unwin
- Miller, D. Beautiful People with beautiful feelings. 2006. Abrams Image
- Rankin, L. Mind Over Medicine: Scientific Proof That You Can Heal Yourself. 2013 Hay House
- Rigg, J. C. Curing the Incurable: How to use your body's natural self healing ability to overcome M.S. and other diseases. 1999 Hara Publishing Group
- Rohn, J. Leading An Inspired Life. 1997. Success Partners Holding Co
- Roosevelt, E. You Learn by Living: Eleven Keys for a More Fulfilling Life. 2009. Westminster John Knox Press
- Vale, J. 7lbs in 7 days: Juice Master Diet. 2014. Harper Thorsons
- Vale, J. The Juice Master: Turbo-charge Your Life in 14 Days. 2014. HarperNonFiction
- Value, J. Seven pounds in seven day. Super juice diet. 2009. HarperCollins Publishers
- Wahls, T MD The Wahls Protocol. 2015. Ebury Digital
- Weiner H. MD Curing MS: How science is solving the mysteries of multiple sclerosis. 2005. Three Rivers Press
- William, A. Medical Medium: Secrets behind chronic and mystery illness & how to finally heal. 2015. Hay House
- Ziglar, Z. See You At The Top. 2002. Magna Publishing

Websites:

- Cheng, C. et al. Prolonged fasting reduces IGF-1/PKA to promote hematopoietic-stem-cell-based regeneration and reverse immunosuppression. 2014. https://pubmed.ncbi.nlm.nih.gov/24905167/
- Farhud, D. & Malmir, M. & Khananmad, M. Health & Happiness: The Biological Factors. 2014. https://www.ncbi.nlm.nih.gov/pmc/articles/PMC4449495/
- Gordon, S. Is Your Healthcare Provider Bullying You During Appointments? 2019. https://www.verywellhealth.com/is-your-doctor-a-bully-4152017
- Macaninch, E. Et al. Time for nutrition in medical education. 2020. British Medical Journal. https://nutrition.bmj.com/content/early/2020/05/05/bmjnph-2019-000049.info
- Marchant, J. How Happiness Boosts The Immune System. 2013. https://pubmed.ncbi.nlm.nih.gov/26060713/
- Newman, K. Six Ways Happiness is Good For Your Health. 2015 https://greatergood.berkeley.edu/article/item/six_ways_happiness_is_good_for_your_health
- Rakin, J. Matthews, L. Cobley, S. Han, A. Sanders, R. Wiltshire, H. Barker, J. Psychological Consequences of Childhood Obesity. 2016. https://pubmed.ncbi.nlm.nih.gov/27881930/
- Socrates. Goalcast: famous quotes from Socrates on life, knowledge and wisdom. https://www.goalcast.com/socrates-quotes/

Suggested Reading

- Brown, L. It's Not Over Until You Win: How to become the person you always wanted to be no matter what the obstacle. 1998. Prentice Hall & IBD
- Dizpenza, J. You Are The Placebo: Making your mind matter. 2014. Encephalon LLC
- Evans, D. Placebo: Mind over matter in modern medicine. 2014. Oxford University Press.
- Hamilton, D. How Your Mind Can Heal You. 2008. Hay House
- Hay, L. You Can Heal Your Life. 1984. Hay House
- Hicks, E. Ask And It Is Given: Learning to manifest your desires. 2004. Hay House
- Hill, N. & Clement Stone, W. Success Through a Positive Mental Attitude. 1959. HarperCollins Publishers
- Lipton, B. et al. The Biology of Belief: Unless the power of consciousness matter and miracles. 2005. Hay House
- Nichols, L. No Matter What: You can overcome every obstacle. 2010 Piatkus
- Nightingale, E. The Strangest Secret. 1956. Nightingale-McHugh Company
- Rohn, J. The Art of Exceptional Living. 1993. Nightingale Co
- Schwartz. D. The Magic of Thinking Big. 2016. Vermilion.
- Scovel-Shinn, F. The Game of Life and How to Play It. 1925. Tarcher Perigee
- Sharma, R. The 5am Club: Own your morning elevate your life. 2018. Harper Thorsons
- Vanzant, I. Tapping the Power Within: A path to self-empowerment for women. 2008. Hay House
- Vincent Peale, N The Power of Positive Thinking. 1990. Cedar Books / Vermilion

About the Author

Carley Mellors-Blair BSc (hons) MRSM MFHT has worked in the Holistic Health industry for 17 years and is the founder of The Healing Touch Academy, Nature's Pharmacy and Altered Health. She has grown from a hands-on body work specialist to a nutritional therapist, to an energy healer, to a 21st Century alchemist. Dedicating her labour of love to the constant proficiency of her craft, she has helped to rebalance and re-energise over 30,000 people through her clinical practice, corporate workshops and seminars, and her national and international wellbeing retreats.

With an academic background in the Social Sciences, Carley has won awards from Loughborough University for her research and carries this thirst for enquiry and understanding into all that she continues to do. Pushing beyond what is known in mainstream medicine, what is taken for granted by society and what has always been accepted, Carley has dedicated her professional career and her personal quest to question more, to know more and to apply what she has learnt as she goes.

Through her own healing journey of reversing Multiple Sclerosis, Carley has had practical experience of functional medicine, epigenetic, neuropsychological, nutritional, and quantum physical approaches to health and wellbeing and presents her findings, not as a PhD research fellow, or a traditionally trained Doctor, but as an ordinary person who wanted to know more.

Over the last decade Carley has built a very busy clinic in Nottingham and has a personal clientele in excess of 3000 people. Her reputation for helping people to heal themselves is such that she now has a 12-week waiting list to see her on a one to one basis. She has a number of corporate clients that she creates workshop and seminars for, from across a range of industries including the National Health Service, the Ikano Bank, The University of Nottingham, Eon, DLA Piper and Cooper Parry, to name but a few. She also launched wellbeing retreats both in the UK and abroad and is now in her 8th year of running these.

With her ethos of helping as many people as she possibly can, Carley shares her story and practical tips from the stage to the classroom. After been invited to present at the Midlands Medical Conference in October 2019, Carley has been approached by Trust Executives to provide a consultation service that will help reframe how we approach chronic and acute pain management. Now as a winner of the Diverse Wisdom Award she has even more drive to share her knowledge and skill with others, which is reflected in her ever growing calendar of speaking engagements.

Would you like to join Carley LIVE at one of her Ways to Wellness events? Work with her on a 1-2-1 basis, or access her online courses?

Register at **www.alteredhealth.co.uk**

Telephone: **+44 (0) 7399 281 950**

Email: **info@alteredhealth.co.uk**

Take Action NOW